Praise for

"This book will help anyone s   t
isn't only about amassing mo   f
growth, vitality, and deeper n.   ~ ~ ...~.p .... ~. ~~ .~~~g....~ that
true wealth comes from embodying enoughness in a personal and more experiential way."
        — **Bari Tessler**, financial therapist and author of *The Art of Money*

"It's rarely about the money. That is the profound truth in Elizabeth Husserl's
brilliant *The Power of Enough*, which explores what really drives and heals
our relationship with security, intimacy, safety, and growth. While money is
important, true fulfillment lies in the experiences that cannot be bought —
vitality, connection, and belonging. This transformative book expands our
notion of wealth and offers a fresh perspective on the infinite game of life,
where quality far surpasses quantity."
        — **Carolyn Buck Luce**, author of *EPIC!: The Women's Power Play Book*

"*The Power of Enough* is an exquisitely crafted guide to redefining our relationship to our most essential ally for thriving: money. Endowing us with a
fundamental way to reframe the scarcity mindset, Elizabeth Husserl grace-
fully examines the choices we make that drain our power, offering practical
and tactical tools for relating to money as a means of fulfilling our highest
expression of wealth. Elizabeth masterfully chaperones us toward an empowering path that leverages resources, time, energy, and attention while
relinquishing biases that prioritize traditional accounts and balances. With
rare and seasoned insight, Elizabeth leaves no stone unturned in precisely
articulating the art of satiation and unearthing the rich rewards that dwell
within our relationships to money and ourselves. A must-read for anyone
interested in optimizing wealth comprehensively while flourishing with un-
paralleled fulfillment and joy."
        — **Krista Kujat**, author of *Life's Poetic Glossary*

"Elizabeth Husserl has written an excellent book that will be of tremendous
value to the financial services industry and her readers. *The Power of Enough*
is filled with beautiful processes that will assist all who wish to explore and
transform their relationship with money. Thank you, Elizabeth, for your
contribution to the field!"
        — **Deborah Price**, CEO and founder of the Money Coaching Institute

"*The Power of Enough* is one of the best personal-finance books I've ever read (and I've read a lot!). While most such books focus on the logistics of money management, Elizabeth Husserl speaks to the joyful purpose and role money can have in our lives if we are brave enough to challenge the conventional wisdom that more is better. In this gem of a book, Elizabeth provides conceptual and tactical ways to take the stress out of your money, helping readers understand at a soul level that financial well-being is where life's true riches can be found. Highly, highly recommend."

— **Manisha Thakor, CFA, CFP**, author of
MoneyZen: The Secret to Finding Your "Enough"

"Transformative. Elizabeth Husserl's unique approach leads you to unpack your relationship with money, define what 'enough' means for you, and be intentional about your core values. This is far more than wealth management — it's happiness management."

— **Karan Singh, COO**, Headspace

"If money stirs your emotional pot, this book is for you. *The Power of Enough* offers a powerfully transformative view of the role money plays in a life worth living. Elizabeth Husserl teaches us, in this fabulously practical guide, how to build and enjoy a wealth of well-being and how to get rich in all the right ways — through joy and fulfillment."

— **Jodi Wellman**, author of
You Only Die Once: How to Make It to the End with No Regrets

"Anyone looking for an antidote to the relentless pursuit of more should read this book."

— **Barbara Huson**, author of
Overcoming Underearning and *Rewire for Wealth*

"Money is often the area where we most need fresh approaches and teachings. *The Power of Enough* offers an abundance of ways to rethink our understanding of money. Redefining 'enough' is in itself more than enough to transform our relationship with money, and yet there are so many additional lessons to be found in this book."

— **Kate Levinson, PhD**, author of *Emotional Currency:
A Woman's Guide to Building a Healthy Relationship with Money*

the POWER of
ENOUGH

the POWER of ENOUGH

finding joy in your relationship with money

ELIZABETH HUSSERL

foreword by LYNNE TWIST

New World Library
Novato, California

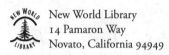

New World Library
14 Pamaron Way
Novato, California 94949

Text design by Tona Pearce Myers

Library of Congress Cataloging-in-Publication data is available.

First printing, January 2025
ISBN 978-1-60868-942-2
Ebook ISBN 978-1-60868-943-9
Printed in Canada

10   9   8   7   6   5   4   3   2   1

New World Library is committed to protecting our natural environment. This book is made of material from well-managed FSC®-certified forests and other controlled sources.

This book is dedicated to my ancestors:
Opa, Oma, Mama Tere, and Papapa,
Kathy Anne, Malidoma, Ruta, and Ramon,
and all those who came before me,
for the wisdom you imparted in my bones,
and for paving the way for new stories of being to be told.

CONTENTS

Part 3: Tools for Embodying Wealth

FOREWORD

This is a challenging time to be alive, and yet perhaps it is the most exciting time in the history of our species. We are living with extreme income inequality, racial and social tensions, a divided political landscape, a crisis in healthcare, rampant depression and mental illness, and a nearly insurmountable climate emergency. It is a polycrisis that has many faces and many dimensions.

People from all sectors and all walks of life are looking deeply at the question of where we have gone off course. Where has humanity misunderstood its role and become such a destructive presence on this planet, constantly accumulating more and more in a way that is driving massive breakdowns and severe unintended consequences?

This book and the profound work of Elizabeth Husserl respond to this at the very heart and core of where we have lost our way. *The Power of Enough* addresses not only our relationship with money, unlimited accumulation, and acquisitions, but also the desperate hunger that lives in the heart and soul of the human family as we try to fill that emptiness with more of anything and everything. Elizabeth is a wise soul who has done her homework — not only out in the world but also in the depths of her own soul. She is the consummate professional and at the same time a fierce and effective warrior of the heart.

For the past thirty years, I have been studying the unconscious, unexamined mindset of scarcity, which drives so much of our dysfunctional behavior. This toxic mindset has us believing that we have to acquire more and more in an endless chase that will never fulfill us or bring us what we're actually looking for. Elizabeth understands this deeply, both personally and professionally. She has looked at it from many different angles and dimensions. After years of reflection and research, she has written a brilliant and deeply insightful and profound book that will alter the very course of the way you live your life.

Sufficiency, satiation, and fulfillment are what people really want — yet we all seem to be hypnotized by the addiction to more. Years ago, I wrote a book called *The Soul of Money*, and since that time, I have seen even more clearly that the enormous climate crisis that we are facing is a direct result of the unconscious, un-examined mindset of scarcity. Our obsession with accumulating "wealth" is so hypnotic that we don't realize what we already have. So we endlessly chase more and more.

Actual wealth, "true" wealth, comes from our well-being. The source or derivation of the word *wealth* is "well-being," and one could say that true well-being actually comes from the "well of being," which is an infinite source for every life. Elizabeth brilliantly unpacks our obsession with wealth and our misunderstanding of abundance, leading us out of the false trance of scarcity.

Read this book and find that place in yourself that is whole, that is fulfilled, that is more than enough, that is satiated and who you really are.

Elizabeth is a shining light in the darkness. May this book expand that light in a way that opens hundreds, thousands, and ultimately millions of people to the fulfillment that's been there all along. Thank you, Elizabeth, for your wisdom, your insight, your courage, and your love.

LYNNE TWIST
Author of *The Soul of Money*

INTRODUCTION

Embracing Wealth as an Experience of Joy

What if I told you one of the fastest ways to create more joy in your life is to turn toward money and see it as a teacher and guide? It is time to talk, both to money and about money. As you search for joy and deeper meaning, money is waiting there, holding an important key. It is an essential ally, always there to guide you as a catalyst for change.

Contrary to popular belief, money is not soulless, nor is it the cause of our cultural or personal ills. Money is a mirror, one of our greatest assets, and a teacher. Like all true mentors, money can be brutally honest. It sees us at our depths, takes us at our word, and holds us accountable to ourselves. If we are going to learn its lesson, we must get curious about what it is trying to teach us. It is going to take courage to peel back the layers of this relationship. And there are riches waiting for you on the other side. If you can integrate what money is ready to reflect, there is a deep and abiding experience of wealth ready to unfold.

But here's the catch and the thing that gets in everyone's way: money is the easiest scapegoat in the world. Each of us has had strong feelings about money at some point in our lives. For some, these feelings surface as visceral hate and dislike. Others experience feelings of being overwhelmed, fearful, or even weighed down by a mountain of grief. I have heard it all. People tell me money has ruined their relationships, betrayed them, and led them to burnout. The stories may differ, but the common denominator remains — money is the cause of their suffering, and capitalism, economics, or any other factor related to wealth and money is to blame.

To get a better sense of how money wants to show up in your life, I want you to join me in a short game of imagination. Imagine that you have been invited to a once-in-a-lifetime opportunity to sit in the presence of a renowned spiritual teacher. This is someone everyone has been talking about. They say this teacher can see who you are at the depths of your soul. They say that when you sit with this person, all your unconscious biases, deeply held values, and secret fears are on display. This sounds a bit intense, but you have heard that this teacher works wonders. They are someone you've been dying to meet, and you can't believe your luck in receiving an invitation.

You arrive to meet this person, but as soon as you see them, your emotions explode. You are livid, angry, and disgusted. You have this feeling that something is wrong with this teacher. You notice that they are paying attention to another group of people, and you experience a level of envy and jealousy you have never felt before. You feel a deep sense of shame, a powerful sensation that you are inadequate and people don't really want you here. You are sad and lonely. You want more than anything to understand your purpose in this life, but being in the presence of this teacher presents so many opportunities that you shut down.

While all this is happening, you find yourself at a loss for words. How could you possibly share such vulnerable things with another person? The teacher smiles back at you, radiating an aura of unconditional acceptance. You notice something odd happening. It is as if you see a mirror image of yourself. You are looking at this teacher, but what you see are the hidden parts of yourself, the ones that have you feeling inundated by emotions you don't even recognize as your own. Just being in the presence of this teacher puts you in contact with parts of life you have been ignoring for years.

You have an impulse to raise your fist and yell at this teacher. How dare they make you feel like this! Who are they to make you feel this way? But then you see them smile. They call you over and ask your name. You agree to sit down and talk. As the conversation unfolds, you realize the feelings are both yours and those inherited from your ancestors. You are still stirred up, but something softens. You realize that your past doesn't define your life as you thought it did. As you tell your story, you feel a renewed sense of agency. There is something about this conversation that makes you feel inspired.

Now imagine that this spiritual teacher is money. What would you say?

Remember, money is the ultimate scapegoat, but it doesn't have to be this way. Money is so much more than we give it credit for. It is in relationship with every person on this planet. It knows what we desire and what we want to push away and ignore. It knows our history better than we do, and it understands the zeitgeist of our contemporary moment in ways we can't imagine. Money is a facilitator of opportunities, a means of expression, and a stimulus for innovation. Through its relationship with us, it has learned to use the incredible amount of data that streams toward it every day. If we turn toward money, we are bound to learn about ourselves and the nuances of the worlds we live in.

And yet, our relationship with money is so energetically charged. It doesn't matter whether you have a lot or a little money; when the topic comes up, it touches something deep and vulnerable in each of us because it represents so much — so much possibility, so much growth, so much meaning. But instead of learning how to develop a healthy relationship with money, we become fixated on accumulating more. But no matter how much money you have, you can't buy meaning. There are few relationships in life as important as the one we have with money, yet we have not been taught how to engage with this important teacher. That's where this book comes in.

The Power of Enough is an invitation to explore a new possibility in your relationship with money and wealth, where money becomes a trusted mentor that pushes you to expand your horizon and wealth becomes something to embody instead of possess. This requires a radical transformation of how we see wealth, how we define money, and the ways we take responsibility for where we've gone wrong.

In part 1 of this book, you embark on a journey to fundamentally redefine your understanding of wealth and money. We take a closer look at the nature of money itself and introduce the powerful practice of sitting down and having a conversation with it. From this foundation, you will begin the journey toward reclaiming your role as the architect of your own financial story. With the help of these tools, you can design your life in conjunction with a more expansive definition of wealth.

In part 2, you delve deeper into the transformative journey of embodying wealth and cultivating a profound sense of satiation in your life. These chapters invite you to move beyond the limitations of the abundance-scarcity cycle and embrace a more expansive, holistic understanding of wealth — one rooted in the rich fabric of your lived experiences and the fulfillment of your deepest needs.

Part 3 invites you to explore what it truly means to embody wealth by inviting money and the wisdom it brings deeper into your life. You will gain tools to discover the wisdom of your money stories, your financial DNA, and the power of unconditional acceptance. These chapters guide you toward a deeply personal and embodied experience of abundance and fulfillment. You then get to decide what to release and what to keep, allowing you to redesign how you want to live. This doesn't happen through judgment, guilt, or failure. It happens with grace, love, and unconditional acceptance, honoring the simple fact that you chose to read this book, which offers the possibility of discovering something new.

The Power of Enough presents a way out of the scarcity mindset that plagues our modern culture. It accomplishes this by examining how we define wealth and money and by sharing tools, practices, and techniques to help you feel the wealth that is a natural ground of your being. These practices help us move past the dominant cultural assumptions around scarcity *and* abundance. Such a journey requires us to shift out of a paradigm built solely on material things. This new world is grounded in experiences of satiation and fulfillment, where encounters with joy and moments of meaning are integrated into our lives.

As we learn the truth about money, we can work our way out of scarcity. This requires some courage on our part, as we need to share our money stories while uncovering our cultural patterns and beliefs. If our stories remain unexamined, our unconscious patterns control us. Awareness gives us the power to choose what is working and what is not. We need to learn how to relate to money in order to truly embody wealth.

Love requires two components: spaciousness and intimacy. *The Power of Enough* is a journey to love yourself, love others, and even love money by finding a healthy relationship with it. We need an intimate connection with money that is infused with honest, authentic conversations not just with people about money but with money itself. We also require the spaciousness to know we are enough, no matter how much money we have in our bank accounts.

This is the other side of financial freedom, where you are deeply rooted in the absolute knowing that you have the capacity to fulfill your needs at every moment. But we need to understand that needs are natural and what they are in the first place.

Our external environment mirrors the imbalance in each of us. We must be willing to dive into our relationship to money and understand our actual desires so that we can satisfy our craving for more. Over the many years I have worked with money, it has become a trusted guide, pointing me toward what I need to take care of and revealing those pesky blind spots that elicit feelings of scarcity and get in my way. I have learned that what I seek is often found within.

I clearly remember the day I realized that if I died tomorrow, I would have lived enough of a life to feel it had been worth it. Standing in my parents' library after a two-year stint of living and working abroad in Oaxaca, Mexico, I found myself searching for a new book to read. A wave of immense satisfaction swept over me. I was flooded with memories from the past two years and felt a sense of knowing that my work had not only been extremely meaningful but also fulfilled some of my most essential human needs.

My time in Oaxaca profoundly marked me. I had been working for a local nonprofit, teaching women about microfinancing and how to start savings and loan cooperatives. I shared practical tools and new ideas, yet what most shaped me was less what I gave and more what I received. I was surprised to discover that the gifts I collected were nonmaterial. They were a hand squeeze from a community elder whose eyes twinkled in gratitude. It was a hug from a participant during a workshop, in appreciation for the information shared. It was the quiet time I spent wandering in local ruins and the sense of collective sacredness I felt when invited by local families to participate in their celebrations for Día de los Muertos. Little did the Oaxacans know that with each hug, smile, and gesture offered, I was recalibrating my experience of well-being, happiness, and wealth, leading me to touch a level of joy that filled my cup of gratitude to its brim.

One afternoon, after finishing a workshop, I went out for a walk to clear my head. I was so engrossed in my thoughts, contemplating the probability of success for these women, that I didn't even notice I was lost. I raised my head and looked around at my surroundings. I recognized nothing. I tried to remember how I had reached the field where I stood. Which grove had I come out of? I didn't know. All the patches of trees looked identical. I tried retracing my steps, but I was met with a sinking feeling. The whole mountainside surrounding the field looked the same. At that moment, a thundering thought struck me: *If I couldn't find my way back and no one came to find me, I wouldn't know how to survive.*

Here I was, obsessing over how to teach Indigenous women to create financial structures, worried that they wouldn't find the discipline to meet their goals. Yet they possessed a skill I did not have. They had the ability not only to survive but to thrive, rooted in their deep relationship to one another and the natural world. The women of this village had a wealth of skills and practical knowledge about living and adapting to their environment, passed down through hundreds of years of human experience. A different face of wealth stared me down, one based on the depth of relationships with others and with nature. I felt a new clarity that chilled me to my bones. *My work wasn't in Oaxaca. I had received what I needed from there. It was time to go home.*

Eventually, one of the Oaxacan villagers found me that day I got lost. I was the subject of much humor that evening, but I simply smiled and owned that the joke was on me. And in the months before I left Oaxaca, I used my visits to the village to interview people so that I could more accurately understand their views on wealth.

The communities in Oaxaca revealed how their wealth was not based solely on how much they saved, made, or achieved. It was equally based on their web of connections and the inner resources that came from facing the triumphs and hardships of life. Rather than wealth being a *thing* to possess and accumulate, their wealth was an *experience* connected to resilience, generosity, health, well-being, and the strength to survive. The inspiration for knowing the power of enough and leading a life of embodied wealth was born.

I once feared that advocating for embodied wealth would come across as unsophisticated and naive. Instead, I discovered that the journey toward embodied wealth is simple and profound. It meant squaring my own relationship with money and taking responsibility for what was standing in my way.

Oaxaca revealed that treating wealth as something to accumulate and money as something to hoard leads to superficial affluence and isolation. Wealth requires relationships — with ourselves, others, our familial line, and the natural and material world we inhabit. It is a two-way street. Embodying wealth entails that we feel at home with ourselves, our stories, and our experiences. When we create a way of life that is grounded in the acceptance and appreciation of who we are, we are better equipped to succeed. And when we understand wealth in this way, we grasp the authentic role of money in our lives.

It has taken me over twenty years to own my transformation with money, and my effort has set me on an amazing journey beyond my wildest dreams. I have traveled through many countries, worked with people across the full spectrum of wealth, sat with beloved teachers, celebrated countless successes, and grieved personal losses as well as those with my clients. The fullness of my life continues to clarify the insight I received in my parents' library many years ago — that I have the power, agency, responsibility, and human right to claim my power of enough. And I have no doubt that you can do this too.

PART 1

Redefining
WEALTH
and
MONEY

Chapter One

REDEFINING WEALTH

Beyond Scarcity and Abundance

For decades, I have been exploring an essential question: Why do we have so much and yet feel so poor? This question took on a life of its own during my two-year stint working in Indigenous villages in Oaxaca, Mexico. It struck me that the people I was working with seemed a lot happier than many of the people I knew back in the United States. I asked the men and women of the village what wealth meant to them. The themes were consistent. Wealth meant health, community, rituals, and celebrations. It meant spirituality and trusting that there was something greater than our human selves to connect to. It meant honoring our elders and embracing the sheer gift of being alive, no matter what hardships we might face. It meant sharing the bounty with fellow villagers, trusting that through your sharing there would be plenty to go around.

As the villagers disclosed their thoughts, I perceived something deeper. Wealth was a shared experience that connected them as a group of people. They had a responsibility to add to the collective field cocreated by their shared currency (which took many forms). They also enjoyed the certainty that comes from a social safety net that would support them in times of need. Wealth was meant not only for individual consumption but also for sharing with the whole community. While people I met in and around Oaxaca did not have a lot of material wealth, they had found a way to integrate the meaningful experiences they had in their lives. In contrast, many of the people I knew back home had an abundance of material resources but seemed to be struggling to feel full. This distinction appeared to make all the difference.

If we look closely at our lives, we need material resources to feel secure — think food, shelter, clothing, healthcare, and savings. All of these add to a sense of safety and protection. To this end, having enough material resources can be an indicator of our *financial health* and *security*. If our car breaks down, we need to know we can afford to fix it. On our child's first day of school, we need to provide healthy food, clean clothing, and school supplies. If a medical emergency happens or we lose our job, we need to know we have a safety net and are going to be OK while we assess the situation. Yet once we have established a baseline of financial health, adding more resources does not necessarily increase our ability to *feel* wealthier, much like better restaurants, bigger homes, and fancier clothing do not equate to greater health and happiness.

At its core, the answer to my original question — Why do we have so much yet feel so poor? — lies in our perception of money and our ability to *experience* wealth while we accumulate it. This is the core premise of the book — wealth is not just about what we have, it is about who we are. For too long we have equated wealth with an amount of money in our bank account, when wealth is all about our sense of well-being. The purpose of wealth is to help us live a more joyful and meaningful life. When you have a clear understanding of your identity and your values, you are rich. Money has a role to play in helping you learn these lessons. While you might amass great quantities of it, you cannot let it define you.

Take a moment to be with this statement and ask yourself, Does money define me? Be honest with yourself and honor whatever you hear. If you have a sense that money defines certain aspects of your life, you are not alone. I am the first to raise my hand and admit I have let money hold unnecessary power over how I view and value myself.

Money alone cannot solve our problems, and having a lot of it does not necessarily make us feel wealthy. Yet money can show us the way. It has taken me decades of working with people and their relationship with money to understand this. Money is not just a tool; it is also a guide. It is an instrument that, when used with awareness and intent, can fulfill your needs, offer support, and help realize your personal and professional ambitions. When you get lost in the cycle of trying to acquire more and more money, you risk missing money's actual role in your life, which we will discover together as we go. The lessons found in this book can help you to reclaim your sense of power and agency in the world. But this does not happen by ignoring or turning away from it. In fact, it requires just the opposite. You need to turn toward money to better understand what it is trying to teach you. In the process, you will transform your experience with wealth and well-being.

Before we go any further, it is important for you to get a sense of your own relationship to wealth. We will use the "mini moments" throughout the book to pause and reflect to help key points sink in. Take a journal and write down the first thoughts and feelings that emerge as you read the questions below.

• MINI MOMENT •

Do I feel truly wealthy in my life right now? Have I ever felt wealthy? If so, in what ways?
Are money and wealth the same thing or different?

Wealth, like beauty, is in the eye of the beholder. By the end of this chapter, I hope you feel the depth of the wealth you carry with you wherever you go.

Wealth Requires More Than Scarce Resources

Typically, we think of wealth as the total market value of our possessions. Take a balance sheet, for example. First, we add our assets (what we own), then we subtract our liabilities (what we owe). The final number gives us a fast calculation of our net worth. If we do a quick online search, one of the first things we read about net worth is that it represents the value of a person or company. No wonder we tie the concept of wealth to self-worth and commodify our sense of value against our balance sheet.

In our modern culture, we define wealth as an accumulation of material resources aimed at generating profit and increasing our bottom line. As the saying goes, "money talks": The more money you have, the wealthier you are and the more power and influence you obtain. This notion floods the popular imagination through music, movies, advertisements, and books on how to get rich quick.

As a financial advisor, I know money is extremely important and deserves our awareness, care, and attention. I help people every day to create a sense of abundance in their lives through developing healthy habits around wealth creation and financial planning. A financially healthy person has a working relationship with how they earn, save, spend, and invest. They can pivot as new challenges emerge and opportunities arise. A financially healthy person can leverage their ability to generate financial wealth to accomplish all kinds of significant things in their life.

Common benchmarks of our financial health include our credit score, the size (or existence) of a rainy-day fund, and home-ownership. These types of material wealth provide access to a greater array of goods and services, afford us stability and security, and give us a starting point from which we turn our goals into reality. Understanding how the financial system works and how to participate in it is crucial for building a strong financial foundation for ourselves. However, when money is used as a stand-in for *all* wealth, we create a society that is affluent on paper yet lacks intimacy and meaning. We fail to recognize that our wealth is also revealed through the strength of our relationships and our sense of purpose and meaning.

Money and wealth are different things. Money is a social technology, which we dive into more deeply in the next chapter. Wealth, in contrast, is a state of *well-being*. Our financial health contributes to our wealth, but our well-being is far more than the sum of our material resources. Conflating money and wealth contributes to a societal paradox: we are rich in assets yet starved for meaning and soul.

Abundance-Scarcity Cycle

The problem is not with wealth per se, but rather with how we conceive it. Since the early twentieth century, economics has been defined as the study of human behavior in relation to how people use, produce, and consume limited resources. It is the science of human decision-making in the material world.

Following this definition, the most common understanding of wealth is the accumulation of scarce resources. This definition unintentionally creates a vicious cycle where the only solution to our sense of scarcity is to continually acquire more.

When we emphasize scarcity, wealth becomes confusing. Its meaning is reduced to having an abundance of material resources that are limited or difficult to obtain. The scarcity of these items is what makes them valuable, and acquiring more of them contributes to our popular concept of wealth. We spend all our time running from scarcity, trying to create a sense of security. We are simultaneously grasping at money and pushing scarcity away. This is not a very hopeful way of living, and it raises a couple of key issues.

First, by focusing only on scarce resources when talking about wealth, we risk reducing all resources to solely material possessions, like money, property, natural resources, forms of financial capital, and various other *things*. This leads us to assume that being rich means owning an abundance of resources, mostly made up of material goods. This view is shortsighted and fosters a perpetual sense of scarcity.

The second issue is subtler and even more important. It has to do with the idea of abundance. People have been writing about abundance and money for a hundred years. Books like those of Wallace D. Wattles (*The Science of Getting Rich*, 1910) and Napoleon Hill (*Think and Grow Rich*, 1937) went a long way toward creating a popular discourse around the role of abundance in our lives. The term *abundance mindset* was coined by Stephen R. Covey in *The 7 Habits of Highly Effective People*. Covey presented this concept to counteract what he called a *scarcity mindset*. Abundance means having more than what you need. He argued that by adopting an abundance mindset, we would come to accept the notion that there are sufficient resources and opportunities for everyone to succeed.

Yet often this swings too far in the other direction, leading us to grasp at abundance while pushing away scarcity. Together, they create an *abundance-scarcity cycle* that can have an outsized impact on our lives and distract us from the bigger question of how much is enough.

The overuse of external resources is real. If we continue to prioritize strategies that emphasize material growth, our economy will eventually both implode and explode. We see it happening now with climate change, overconsumption, and overpopulation. Our world is both heating up and flooding over at the same time. Our external environment mirrors the imbalance within each of us, forcing us to ask, Have we gone too far?

If we consider our current definition of success within the abundance-scarcity cycle, the more assets we have, the wealthier and more successful we are. The more we earn, the higher our net worth. As a society, we buy into the misguided assumption that our intrinsic self-worth is determined by our net worth. Regardless of whether we realize it, we mistakenly think we are trapped in this scarcity cycle. We also believe that money is responsible for either getting us out of or keeping us in this position.

No wonder we all have so much emotion around money and finances. In this world of scarce resources, the only way to have more self-esteem is to get more money. In this scenario, our sense of self becomes tied to the ups and downs of our bank accounts. When we align our need for well-being to the accumulation of material resources alone, we mistakenly believe that our experience of wealth needs to come from an external source. We place money and profit above all else. And here is the funny thing: No amount of abundance of scarce resources can get us out of this mess. An abundance mindset cannot solve the problem of scarcity; they are opposite poles of the same cycle.

If we blindly play the game of accumulating scarce resources, we will never realize the power of enough. If we keep buying into the collective fallacy that our worth as a person is equal to the amount of material resources we have accumulated, we risk conflating money and profit with people and purpose.

The pursuit of money for the sake of making more money makes us feel like we are stuck in a vicious cycle. Well-being cannot be purchased, yet we keep going back to try to buy more. It's no surprise we are all exhausted by our relationship with money and our never-ending race for new things. The good news is that there is a way out. The path forward comes in three parts: first we need new definitions, then we need new practices and tools, and finally we need to create a new relationship with money that supports us in embodying wealth along the way.

I invite you to challenge the modern tale you have been told about money. In taking this step, you might just find that money is more of a companion and a guide, rather than a guardian at the gates of some mythical utopia where everyone is fulfilled because of their bank accounts.

The Infinite Game: Wealth and Well-Being

The etymological root of wealth comes from the word *well-being*. I see this connection popping up more and more in contemporary conversations about wealth and money. We are starting to understand that wealth disconnected from well-being misses the mark. It speaks to the sentiment many of us have that our relationship to money and wealth feels somewhat "off," but we can't quite find the source of this unease.

Willpower alone can't change how we feel about money. We can't think our way out of scarcity. Nor can we simply practice abundance thinking or visualize wealth and have it magically appear. Instead, we need to learn how to *embody* our wealth, which will change our relationship to it. Put simply, we need to find concrete ways to experience wealth from the inside out, using both material and experiential resources to build our relationship to money, transforming it into a guide to well-being.

• MINI MOMENT •

What's the first thing that comes to mind when I imagine money?
What does it look and feel like?

Now that you have a better understanding of your own thoughts on wealth and money, let's take a closer look at what these two concepts are all about.

Philosopher James P. Carse introduced an important distinction between what he called *finite* and *infinite* games. In a finite game, there is a clear beginning and an end, and the goal is to win. In an infinite game, the goal is to continue playing, and participants can focus more on the journey and process, which are key ingredients of both joy and sustained fulfillment.

Because infinite games have no beginning or end, they are also more flexible. Rules change over time, and the game adapts to new contexts and environments. Players are incentivized to inspire and encourage others to both join the game and do well in it. They are motivated to concentrate on long-term development, rather than on short-term success, and their focus becomes more about growth, learning, and creativity, as opposed to the competition and scarcity prevalent in finite games.

Our contemporary approach to work and retirement is the perfect example of a finite scenario. Work is seen as something you can eventually win — I have saved enough money that I have won the game, and so I can stop playing (i.e., I can retire). Retirement in this context looks like stepping out of the game of life. Retired people can enjoy a life of leisure, which in this context is the goal. While large numbers of millennials race to win the game and retire as soon as possible, a huge population of retired people find themselves adrift, with no obvious new game to play.

If we saw our work as one part of a larger, infinite game, this entire structure would change. In an infinite game, the idea is to adapt to new situations while we engage in a lifelong practice of developing ourselves. Retirement doesn't make sense in this scenario. The goal is not to sacrifice your quality of life today only to save enough money to have the quality of life you want after retirement. The act of saving can still be important, but the ultimate focus shifts toward the present moment, with the primary goal being understanding what strategies, investments, and decisions support your long-term flourishing and development. Our relationship to money is part of an infinite game in which the goal is continual participation and ongoing transformation.

When you lean into a growth mindset, you understand that life is fluid and believe that your intelligence, abilities, and qualities can evolve and improve with dedication and commitment. You view effort and perseverance as essential for learning any new skills and see hard work as the bedrock for achieving success. You find inspiration in the success of others and commit yourself to creating a meaningful life by seeking fulfillment.

In contrast, when you are playing a finite game, you tend to be in a fixed mindset. You work hard at maintaining your static identity. I am a person who works and will eventually retire. The goal is to win (i.e., retire), yet life is an unwinnable game. If you are worried about winning, you tend to avoid challenges, fearing that failures today will mean you can't retire in the future. This fixed mindset is at the heart of the finite game around wealth and money that so many people play. If the only resources you have available to you are scarce, there is obviously competition for them, and whoever has more at the end of the day wins. In this reality, people feel threatened by the success of others, believing that it diminishes their own worth.

The game of life is not fixed or finite. It is not about competing for scarce resources. Having more things than other people does not count as a win. Life is an infinite game about creating wealth and well-being, not just for us but for everyone in our community, including everyone in the world. There are a lot of important resources in our lives that are not material or scarce. This distinction is crucial. Material resources, physical labor, and financial capital are scarce and thus *finite*. But our well-being and our ability to experience wealth is *infinite*.

To feel truly wealthy, we need to move past a definition of resources based on quantity and abundance — how much we have — and toward a definition of resources based on quality and meaning — how much we can develop and grow. This important step helps us define ourselves based on who we are today, rather than what we have saved for our retirement tomorrow.

Creating an abundance of resources only addresses areas in our lives where issues of scarcity and quantity come into play. This is why retirement feels so daunting for many people. They have sacrificed their own growth and happiness to be able to devote time to themselves later. By the time there are finally enough resources to retire, it is often too late to focus on personal development.

Accumulating more stuff creates security, while integrating more meaning leads to satiation. Both are important, but we get stuck in the abundance-scarcity cycle while trying to address security, forgetting that the purpose of wealth is to create a state of well-being, which is found through learning what experiences and relations fill you up. We postpone our well-being in the present, with the goal of making enough money so that we can focus on our well-being in the future. But retirement is just one among the many examples we could use.

Modern definitions of economics are stuck in an abundance-scarcity cycle to the extent that they emphasize the accumulation of scarce resources as the primary marker of wealth. To this end, they are playing a finite game of quantity over quality. The goal of this book is to teach you how to embody wealth so that you can appreciate the profound experience of your unique power of enough and consequently feel more joy. That said, these words are a little abstract, so let's take our first steps toward your own experience of the power of enough.

Three Simple Steps to Embody Wealth in Your Life

The power of enough is fundamental to your natural state of being. The simple practice below can ensure that you learn how to integrate this abundance of meaning into your life.

Your body requires energy to thrive, and a lot of this energy comes through the food you eat. When you are mindful about health and nutrition, and bring awareness to the foods you consume and how your body digests them, it is easier to transform what you eat into the energy needed to live a healthy and vital life. Similarly, when you take time to consciously digest meaningful experiences, including those with money, you fill yourself up.

You embody meaning by digesting it. Meaning is then turned into resources that can be used or stored, creating a deep well of satisfaction you can draw on today or in the future. In this well of satiation, you access the innate reserve that is the power of enough. But the question still arises, How do you do this? How do you digest the moments of meaning that naturally arise for you?

Here is a simple three-step process to ensure that you can integrate the significant experiences in your life:

1. *Recognize* and *appreciate* each moment of meaning that nourishes you.
2. *Digest* these moments of meaning by *integrating* what nourishes you and *releasing* whatever your body doesn't need.
3. *Satiate* yourself with these experiences. Allow these moments of meaning to accumulate and *compound*, creating a sense of innate fulfillment that connects you to the deep well of your own unique expression of the power of enough.

Step 1: Recognize and Appreciate

Every day presents an opportunity to be in exchange with others, nature, what you produce and consume, and ultimately yourself. Pay attention to the moments that have the greatest impact. They can be positive or challenging. They can be big or small. What matters is to take the time to recognize and appreciate them as important successes on your journey. This is the first step toward living a life with more joy.

Step 2: Digest through Integrating and Releasing

To digest the meaningful moments in our lives, we must fully experience and process them. This is an important point. If you don't take the time to recognize and appreciate these moments, they may not get digested. This is especially true for highly charged moments that we experience as either incredibly positive or particularly challenging. These experiences can feel like they are too much, as they challenge us to transform our perception of ourselves.

Consumption is an economic act that, in itself, is neither good nor bad. It is the act of using resources to satisfy needs and wants. We can apply values to what we consume, but the act of consumption is neutral. Yet it still plays an important role in embodying wealth. By digesting these impactful moments, we can consume the potential energy they provide. And depending on your individual makeup, you will find that some moments are digested and integrated, contributing to your embodied wealth, while others are released because they do not meet your needs or no longer serve a purpose.

Step 3: Compound Meaning, Create Satiation

Over time, moments of meaning start to compound. In the words of Lynne Twist, author of *The Soul of Money*, "What you appreciate, appreciates." The more you can recognize, appreciate, and digest the impactful moments in your life, the more embodied wealth you compound. Similar to how asset allocation creates diversity in an investment portfolio, embodying wealth requires actively discovering the strategies that meet your needs and the ability to rebalance those strategies over time.

Compounding is earning interest on interest — the effect magnifies the returns on your initial investment over time. This is the "miracle of compounding." Similarly, compounding meaning creates satiation, a feeling of satisfaction that stems from having enough and being enough. Meaning begets meaning and allows you to see new possibilities and make important connections. As you shift your focus from external validation to internal satisfaction, you launch a new journey where building wealth includes adding more vitality, connection, and opportunities for growth and purpose into your life.

Take a moment to conjure up a recent experience where you felt satisfied. It can be a big accomplishment or something as simple as pausing and feeling sunlight on your skin. Don't edit yourself on what first shows up.

Now take a moment to *recognize* and appreciate that experience. This allows you to completely feel the moment, giving you an opportunity to *digest* its meaning. Remember, some experiences will be nourishing and will be integrated as embodied wealth, while others will be *released* so that they no longer take up space for you. As meaning is digested, it starts to *compound*, creating an experience of satiation that connects us to our unique power of enough.

PRACTICE: ## Fill Your Cup

Step 1

Take the moment that emerged above. Recognize and appreciate the impactful experience. Pay attention to the elements converged to make this moment meaningful. Who was present? Where were you? How did you feel?

Step 2

Digest and either integrate or release the experience. Integrate by staying with the memory and importance of this moment, allowing space for its impact to expand and grow within you.

Release by consciously exhaling the parts of the experience that need to be let go of. Use your breath to push it out of your body and release it back into the world. Be intentional with your insight. I invite you to literally conjure the moment of this experience and swallow, allowing its meaning to reach every cell in your body.

Step 3

Now imagine this moment *compounding* inside of you. It doesn't matter whether you choose to integrate or eliminate. Choice is agency and agency is self-efficacy, the belief that we have the power to affect an outcome.

Let your choice reveal its meaning as if it were added to the balance sheet of your life, building a well of *satiation* and connecting you to your core.

Breaking Our Habits of Scarcity

When I do this practice for myself, I think about how my relationship to money has changed over the years. I've always taken pleasure in tracking my finances. Balancing my checkbook is a lifelong habit that I enjoy to this day. Yet I've come to realize that there is a fine line between meticulous tracking and obsessive fixation. This recognition has helped me clarify the distinction and digest a new story about money in my life.

For example, in the past, when flying back from a vacation, I'd feel this intense desire to log in and settle my credit card statements before landing. I disliked high balances on my credit cards and wanted to make sure that they didn't stick around. I also felt the need to know exactly how I had spent, because without this information, I felt out of control.

The true cost of my habit was not in the act itself, but in how it rushed me past recognizing all the amazing times I had while on vacation. Because I was not taking the time to recognize these experiences, I was not celebrating them, and I certainly was not digesting them. Balancing my checkbook was not a neutral act; it stemmed from an earlier time in my life when careful budgeting was essential during the beginning of my career. My habit was tied to an undercurrent of scarcity and apprehension that was affecting me in negative ways.

Notice how there was a story about needing to quickly eradicate debt and exercise control. This insight was still a moment of meaning, with important lessons to teach me. It is one that fell into the category of being challenging and needed to be digested and eliminated from my life.

As I recognized this habit for what it was — a challenging story, a moment of meaning, that was negatively affecting me — I learned to ease my grip and let go of control. While the stories I told myself were having a negative impact, the act of recognizing them helped me to disentangle myself from their influence. These stories had not been digested, and so they had not been eliminated. Facing these stories head-on allowed me to digest them. In this case, it was clear that they needed to be removed from my life.

In this way, I was able to compound a new kind of meaning in my life. I was in a place where the scarcity and anxiety that had haunted me for years no longer had anything to teach me. In an earlier time, these had been important teachers. But things had changed, and I had not taken the time to recognize, appreciate, and digest the new story I was in. This process was an important step on my journey toward embodied wealth. I was able to compound this meaning to add to the ongoing sense of satiation in my life.

Now I have new habits that align better with where I am in my journey. To relive the highlights of our trip, my husband, daughter, and I intentionally set aside time, either on the last night of our vacation or while waiting for the plane to take us home. As a result, I've found that when flying home from vacations, I am more inclined to immerse myself in music, gaze out at the clouds, or engage in creative writing. This helps me embrace not only a sense of gratitude but also a profound feeling of satiation and fulfillment. Because I digested and eliminated the old stories while integrating new moments of meaning into my life, I can savor the fresh memories, allowing them to fully saturate my senses.

• MINI MOMENT •
What habit around scarcity no longer serves me?

Requiring Less to Feel More

As we redefine wealth in this way and follow the steps laid out above, we experience what at first seems like a paradox — satiation and the power of enough require fewer resources to feel more well-being. Rather than offering mere financial wisdom or suggesting that the path to joy is found by turning away from material concerns, I suggest you try this transformative approach to experiencing deep satisfaction through recognizing and understanding the patterns, stories, and beliefs we hold regarding money. But here is the key: This is done *while in relationship to money* and the material world. Depth and wealth are equally important, and they can coexist.

When we savor meaningful moments and arrive at the power of enough, we nourish ourselves in ways that are fundamentally different from what we were taught about money, wealth, and economics. The journey toward your power of enough involves consciously recognizing, appreciating, and digesting these moments so that they compound to form a robust state of embodied wealth. This kind of wealth is grounded in feelings of satiation and connected to your power of enough. In essence, this book provides sustenance for all parts of you, guiding you to a wealth that is felt, lived, and grown.

Within Buddhist philosophy, there is a poignant allegory of the "hungry ghost." These beings have insatiable appetites, represented by vast stomachs paired with narrow throats, and find themselves in a never-ending cycle of hoarding and consuming. They are forever cursed by their hunger for more. No matter how much they consume, satisfaction eludes them, and their existence is marred by an unquenchable thirst.

A life of embodied wealth is fundamentally different. It's steeped in moments of significance that we take the time to digest. The three-step process outlined above keeps us present and engaged, allowing us to integrate the nourishing experiences in our lives and eliminate the ones that no longer have meaning for us. These instances hold the power to shape our perspective, strengthen our connections, and invigorate us with vitality, connection, opportunities for growth, and purpose. If we don't take the time for integration and release, we end up in a never-ending cycle of hunger for more.

Embodying moments of meaning creates well-being. Imagine a society that not only discusses strategies for diversification and allocation in our investments but also dives into strategies for recognizing, appreciating, and digesting the meaning, depth, and dimension that these investments bring into our lives. By bridging the gap between the accumulation of wealth and the integration of meaning, you unlock a more profound and purposeful existence, which can start today.

Chapter 1 Takeaways

Redefining Wealth through Growth and Meaning: Traditional definitions of wealth typically focus on the accumulation of scarce resources. If we shift our perspective and redefine wealth as amassing moments of abundance, growth, vitality, and meaning, we recognize that true wealth comes from experiences that resonate on a deep level. Wealth reflects quality over quantity, encompassing not only material possessions but also our emotions, thoughts, relationships, and spiritual insights. Wealth, when seen through this lens, aligns with well-being.

We Are Playing an Infinite Game: There is an important difference between playing a finite game, where the objective is to win, and an infinite game, where the goal is to continue playing and evolving. Infinite games embrace growth, creativity, and long-term development, reflecting a more realistic and sustainable approach to life.

Abundance-Scarcity Cycle: This cycle refers to the pattern where individuals attempt to overcome a perceived lack of resources (scarcity) by accumulating an excess of material goods (abundance). However, this accumulation often fails to address underlying needs for depth and meaning, leading to a continuous and unsatisfying pursuit of more scarce resources.

The Power of Enough: The power of enough is about recognizing and appreciating that what we have in our lives is sufficient for our contentment, happiness, and satiation. It acts as a powerful antidote to the relentless pursuit of more, offering a path to fulfillment that relies not on external accumulation but on internal appreciation. To draw from the power of enough, we learn to compound our moments of satisfaction and find joy in the ordinary. It involves a mindset shift from scarcity to abundance — a realization that wealth is not about having everything, but rather about finding meaning in everything we have. When we tap into the power of enough, we liberate ourselves from the insatiable desire for excess and open to the richness of life that is already ours.

Chapter Two

REDEFINING MONEY

A Social Technology

Defining money is notoriously hard to do. In her book *The Soul of Money*, Lynne Twist writes, "Money is the most universally motivating, mischievous, miraculous, maligned, and misunderstood part of our contemporary life." This sentence probably touches on several reasons why you picked up this book, and it may even strike a nerve. Money has an outsized impact on us. It can feel wildly exhilarating in one moment and downright confusing in the next. Yet we rarely take the time to consider what it is.

What Is Money?

Seeing money as a technology or a tool can help us learn more about the meaning of wealth. When you know who you are and how you fit into your larger community, you have the necessary resources to feel rich. Money has a role to play as you learn who you are, but it cannot define you.

Ultimately, money is a tool with important functions, not an end in itself. And as a tool, money can reflect the actions, beliefs, and values of the person using it in the world. It can communicate important nonverbal messages, especially with people we don't know yet, symbolizing access, status, power, and trust.

Yet many of the strongest emotions we direct toward money are about other things in our lives. Money is a teacher whose mirrorlike qualities can provide profound lessons about how we feel about ourselves and the world around us. Take a moment to consider these statements and ask yourself the following questions. Be honest with yourself and honor whatever you hear.

> • MINI MOMENT •
>
> Does money define me? Has it ever defined me? If so, in what ways?
> Do I have strong emotions or stories about money? If yes, what are they?

Typically, we define money as a medium of exchange and visualize it in the form of either coins or banknotes. Yet if we go way back to around 350 BCE, Aristotle offered a more robust version of this idea. He said that money has four main functions.

First, money is a measure of value. It helps determine the prices of goods and services that we produce and consume. Second, it is a medium of exchange, allowing us to buy and sell resources with one another. Third, it is a store of value. This allows us to save value now, which can be exchanged in the future for other goods and services that we might require at that time. Lastly, money is a method of deferred payment, allowing us to acquire on credit things we cannot afford in full (like a college degree or a house), with the promise to pay lenders back at a future date.

When we use these definitions of money, wealth is reduced to the idea of having the means to purchase, exchange, and produce what we need to support our material life, now and in the future. To thrive in this world, we all need some level of financial stability. And yet, this conception of wealth can feel lacking, as it keeps us in a finite game where money is a scarce resource. It doesn't satisfy the question of what money truly is or why its presence in our lives is so confusing. More importantly, it doesn't highlight the role of money in helping us grow and evolve.

Defining Money as a Social Technology

Let's go back to the definition of money and focus on two things: money as a medium of exchange, and the notion that money comes in the form of coins or banknotes. Both functions are clearly ingrained in our collective psyche, but the second one is not necessarily true. Money does not need to be a finite, physical thing. If I were to ask my teenage daughter what money is, she would likely point to a dollar bill, even though she rarely uses one. My daughter and her generation might associate money with banknotes, but most of the money they use is found in an app on their phone or in the cloud.

Throughout its history, the form money has taken has been malleable. Long before coins or bills were invented, humans used shells, feathers, clay, and beans as physical currency. Most of these items had little or no intrinsic value beyond their agreed-on use as money. This might seem like just another odd fact, one that we have all heard before. But if we look a little closer, the nature of money comes into view in new and interesting ways.

The earliest known use of shell beads occurred over 115,000 years ago, when Neanderthals in southern Spain painted shells to create beaded necklaces. Sites in Israel and southern Africa show that *Homo sapiens* were also creating shell beads to signify social status. Other research suggests that shell necklaces may have been used as money as early as 6000–5500 BCE throughout Europe and around 1000 BCE in China, the South Pacific, North America, South Asia, and West Africa, again to denote status and social rank. It is no surprise that we use jewelry, clothes, shoes, and other material possessions to indicate social standing. As a means of indicating status, money provides insights into why items like shell necklaces evolved to become some of our first forms of currency. These examples demonstrate that money does not need to be tied to some valuable substance. Instead, money holds value because it signifies status, which in turn allows us to create trust by communicating attributes like reliability, credibility, and expertise.

Money has changed forms many times and will continue to do so because it is a financial and relational tool that we readily use and collectively agree on. Its growing emphasis on digitalization highlights the fact that money cannot be equated to valuable *things* or reduced to gold or silver. It is not an item that you hold in your hand. Money is a *social technology* that helps assign value and create and maintain relationships. It has specific functions, but there is no specific form it must take. Both the use and form of money are subject to constant evolution.

This is a radical reframing that can free us from the finite game where money is a scarce resource to hoard in a competitive arena of winners and losers. As we turn toward the infinite game, money is no longer confined to finite forms like coins and banknotes. Instead, when understood as a social technology whose form can adapt to different contexts, it can reveal new avenues of social engagement. This allows us to adjust to novel situations and modify the form of money as needed.

For example, when inflation and bad governance threatened to destroy the monetary system in Argentina in the late 1990s and early 2000s, communities developed their own money by creating pieces of paper called *redes de trueque*, which were used by 2.5 million people across the country. During the Great Depression in the United States, a variety of alternative currencies called scrips were used. Today, there are some six hundred alternative currencies currently in use in Japan. These examples show that once we agree as a group that something is money, that's what it is. Money is valuable to the extent that we agree it is valuable.

Credit as Social Currency

Aristotle followed a similar line of thought. During his time, coins were mostly made of precious metals, so he played with the idea that money had an intrinsic value that lay in the metal itself. People might have wondered whether the silver and gold content in their coins matched the value of the precious metals from which they were made. Aristotle laid the groundwork for defining money as a social tool when he recognized that its value as *currency* depended on law or societal agreement, not just its material composition. Money doesn't have an intrinsic value; rather, we agree on its value to participate and engage with one another.

How can I trust that this money is real and has any value? How can I trust that others will recognize its value and accept it? How can we trust ourselves and others in the creation and management of it? It is fascinating to note that the questions you ask yourself when you meet someone new are exactly the same. Can I trust them? Can I trust that they will do what they say? Are they part of my cultural tribe, or are they part of some other group? Will they be there when I need them? The connection between trust and money runs deep, which leads us to the topic of *credit*, one of the four main functions of money.

Credit comes from the Latin verb *credere*, "to trust." It literally translates to "he/she/it believes." Credit, in its most basic form, points to the trust one person has in the reliability of another and our ability to trust one another. If I provide a service or product to this person today, will they reciprocate the favor later? Once you prove you have good financial credit, a bank believes you will consistently make payments on your car or house. We could say that credit is both a social and a financial tool. A quick look at your current credit score will give you a numerical sense of how responsible and trustworthy the current economic system believes you to be.

Credit existed long before money was invented. Our need to trust one another is fundamental, not just for our financial health but for our overall well-being. A day in our modern lives is characterized by encountering more strangers than our ancestors could have ever imagined meeting in their entire lifetimes. As we walk into this complex web of relationships, how can we figure out who to trust? The answer is money and the credit it provides.

Money can be used to solidify relationships with loved ones, but it does not define or maintain them. It is when we take a few steps beyond these intimate connections that money becomes crucial for situating ourselves within a broader social web. Once we step outside our circle of family and friends, it is important to establish trust and signal our social value, and this is where money plays an essential role. We pay people a salary in exchange for their work. We put our money where our mouth is by contributing to causes we care about and funding organizations dear to our hearts, even if they are geographically distant. Money is exchanged for goods and services with people we might never meet.

What happens when I need to build trust with people I barely know? I must find ways to gauge a person's credit and trustworthiness beyond what I currently know about them. This led us to use credit and money as a stand-in for personal worth. This is why money can feel so confusing. The price of something is determined by supply and demand, but it also reflects what we value. For example, if we charge more or have more, we equate that with high self-worth. This *feels* true because money, trust, and money's function as a store of value are so deeply intertwined. We use money as a gauge of another person's level of value, but we mistakenly allow money to reflect our own worth as well. By default, wealth used in this way is a stand-in for social health, social status, and trustworthiness.

It's no mystery why some of the most common feelings people have about money are confusion, anger, greed, and shame. We want money not just to acquire things and experiences but also to feel more valuable and valued. Money and personal worth have been conflated for some time now.

Many of us equate not having money with having less social status or cachet. This connection is deeply ingrained in our bodies and psyches. But that doesn't mean we have to stay there. If we go back to the three simple steps of embodying wealth outlined in chapter 1, we can conceive of a new relationship with money that is based less on acquiring possessions and social status and more on recognizing, digesting, and integrating our experiences with the material world. Consider this an invitation to discover your true self and realize that you are already enough.

> ● MINI MOMENT ●
>
> In what ways do I use money as a gauge of my sense of self-worth?

How Social Currency Creates Abundance

Let's take a moment to ask, Where did the notion of economics come from? Does it just mean the allocation of scarce resources, or does it mean something different? We can look at three related words from classical Greek to get a clearer sense of its origin.

First, *oikos* refers to a house or household, *oikeioi* represents the members of the household, and *oikonomia* is the management of the household. Put together, we have the ingredients for a deeper meaning of economics based on an interconnected web of relationships that prioritize the health and well-being of the home. While most definitions of economics focus on the connection between the *oikos* (household) and the *oikonomia* (management of the household), it is necessary to examine more closely the *oikeioi*. In the classical Greek context, this word indicated not only close family members but also extended relatives and close friends, which today we might describe as our chosen family.

Contrary to popular belief, traditional cultures seldom used barter systems. "Barter economies rarely existed in the real world," writes Mikael Fauvelle. "Exchanges of goods stemming from the coincidence of wants simply do not take place." People did not barter with their intimate circle of friends and family. In small groups, there was a culture of debt and reciprocity. If you have a basket I need, you might give it to me with the mutual understanding that I am now indebted to you. When you need something from me in the future, you trust I will repay the debt. We rarely barter with one another. Instead, trust is the currency beneath the exchange.

Our best research shows a similar pattern in traditional communities. They did not use barter systems. And the research also shows that bartering was not a common form of social interaction in wider contexts either. If I live in a traditional culture and I require services from someone outside my close circle, I would not barter with them. I would use forms of money as currency as a way to create a system of credit. If I give you this money, I can trust you will show up and provide the agreed-on service.

Take a moment to think about all the things you get from those closest to you. What are the most important aspects of these relationships? How do you show up, and what are your expectations for giving and receiving within your most intimate circles? Do you need money to maintain these relationships? The answer will likely be no. These people know who you are without needing money or achievement-based evidence.

Now imagine that this close-knit group is living together in a small village. Most of your day-to-day needs are met through collaborative effort. As a group, you grow your own food, make your own clothes, and build and maintain your own homes. Everyone has a pretty good understanding of your wealth in the form of social credit. They know what material resources you have, how reliable you are, and the kind of person you are.

Notice that most of your time is spent living and working next to this group of people. This level of engagement and understanding goes beyond basic financial health. You have intimacy, and this shared connection and closeness is its own kind of wealth. You trust that when a challenging situation arises, your family and close friends will be there for you. Your intimate relationships provide you not only security and health but also well-being.

Money was invented to extend our relationships beyond this intimate group and to increase financial and social health beyond the confines of our immediate tribe. It was not a substitute for relational well-being or intimacy.

In modern times, financial health can solve a lot of problems related to security, but it can't tackle problems related to intimacy. Money can expand our influence and relationships beyond our close circle, but it cannot create deep relationships. This distinction is key. Money opens doors for you, but it can't define you once you cross those thresholds. This is where people get it wrong — they let money define them and their sense of worth, conflating money with their personal value. It is a vicious status cycle that is impossible to break. For 99.99 percent of us, someone will always have more material wealth than we do.

Money is like a mirror. It reflects your own insecurities back to you. If you are angry or overwhelmed by money, this may indicate that you are angry at or overwhelmed by something else. It is a neutral tool that makes our values, beliefs, and actions more transparent to those around us. It was invented to create credit (i.e., trust) among people who did not know one another. It was not invented to create intimacy between strangers. Intimacy must be cultivated over time. Money was invented to help us create connections, not intimacy, with people we don't know.

So money is both a tool to help us create working relationships and a mirror that reflects our values and fears. Modern people are far more isolated than our ancestors. When our ancestors created money, they were worried about security rather than intimacy. They used money to widen their connections with people outside their intimate circles. This allowed them to create working relationships, which in turn helped them increase their sense of stability in their lives. Within their close-knit groups, they didn't need money to clarify or maintain their relationships. For the most part, they could trust that the people in their lives would be there when needed. Our ancestors could take their sense of belonging for granted, as they rarely traveled beyond the boundaries of their communities. A person living within relatively constrained borders generally has a clear role and sense of purpose within their tribe.

In today's culture, we have far more opportunities. We can envision almost any job or role for ourselves and make it happen. At the same time, our communities are less cohesive. Remember, money is a mirror that reflects both our values and our fears. As modern people, we are lost in a sea of possibility. Our purpose is not clear, so we try to use money to solve this problem. We tell ourselves that if we just made enough money, we would finally figure it out. At the same time, we don't have as strong a sense of belonging as our ancestors, so we use money to solve this problem, too, telling ourselves that if we just had enough money, that group of people would accept us.

Our modern lives leave us desperate for the kind of meaning that comes from having intimate relationships and a clear sense of purpose. But you can't buy meaning. You can use money to create relatively superficial connections with people you don't know. Some of these connections may become lasting friendships. Some may lead you to a new job, city, or adventure that you never imagined possible for someone like you.

Traditional people may have struggled within their intimate relationships, but they almost always had them. Until very recently, people could assume they would always have the kind of wealth and well-being — trust, belonging, and purpose — that creates meaning for us. Financial health can solve a lot of problems having to do with security, but it can't tackle problems having to do with a lack of meaning.

Money was invented to purchase an abundance of scarce resources so that we could feel secure. Yet we live in a world where there are more resources than we could have imagined even fifty years ago. So why do we feel like we are lacking? The more we try to buy meaning, the more desperate we become. So what good is money in this modern context? To be wealthy, you need a foundation of security. But once your basic needs are met, you must frame your use of money in a very different way.

You cannot buy true friendship. But you can use money to help you engage with people in a diversity of ways. You can't purchase a purpose. But you can pay for a college degree, fund a yearlong sabbatical, attend a workshop, or change jobs to explore a new career. Money can be used to help you get into meaningful situations. But it can't take you all the way. It can't experience the meaning for you. You must embody that on your own. Money can provide an abundance of opportunities, but it is on you to integrate and compound meaning to ensure it becomes a part of your life.

Addressing issues of security is about creating an abundance (i.e., quantity). Solving for things like love and vitality is about compounding meaning (i.e., quality). You need money to create social credit with people you don't know. This is about quantity. Having a lot of social media followers or a big email list does not lead to social belonging. Belonging is about meaning and quality. We live in a world of likes, follows, and friend requests. The more likes you have, the better you think you should feel. But life doesn't work like that.

Money is a guide and a mirror. If you buy clothes solely to take pictures to add to your social media profile and get more "friends," money will be there to reflect this back to you. If you buy a gift for a friend going through a hard time to remind them that you are there, money will be there to reflect this back to you. Money creates social currency that can be used to find meaning. It can help you create situations where you can have impactful experiences. But it doesn't provide meaning on its own; it can only offer you reflections.

• MINI MOMENT •

What do I tend to spend my money on? What mirror is money holding up for me through these purchases?

The Scarcity of Intimacy in Our Modern Lives

Creating intimacy takes time, not money. Your intimate relationships tend to give you a sense of trust, belonging, and purpose. I trust the people I am closest with because I have been with them through all sorts of challenging situations. I have a sense of belonging because we have grown closer as we have shared our lives. Within this group, I also have a sense of purpose. I have learned my role in their lives and gained a sense of self-esteem through this process. I uncovered my purpose through my participation. Our sense of trust, belonging, and purpose is fundamental to our well-being. And no amount of money can generate these for us.

Money can facilitate some of these interactions. I love it when my husband buys me flowers, but this is not why I love him. Or as a dear friend recently reflected when I asked why redefining wealth was important, "Wealth for me is having the inner strength and community to support me when I am feeling 'less than.' It means having people to turn toward to share in challenges and successes. It means having people who will listen, hold my joy, and catch me when I fall. It reminds me I am not alone through it all — the good, the bad, and the in-between. This is my circle of wealth."

We all know what it feels like to buy certain clothes to fit into a group (e.g., purchasing designer jeans or a jersey for a team you love). On a superficial level, this creates a sense of belonging, but it is shallow and precarious. Real belonging and trust require you to spend time with people, building relationships that create intimacy, regardless of the clothes you wear. Wearing a jersey can provide a cue to those around you that you all have the same favorite team. This superficial act may give you a sense of belonging, which in turn allows you to show up more fully in this group. But well-being requires a deeper sense of connectedness than can be provided by wearing a shared uniform. To be truly integrated into a group, you need to feel free to be vulnerable and share your true colors. This is what fosters the deep sense of belonging that is essential to connecting wealth and well-being.

The fact that we cannot buy intimacy is obvious, yet we still forget. Why does this happen? Recent research on modern people gives us a window into the reality of our brains. We are wired to compare ourselves to others, and as a result, we get the false idea that buying and sharing stuff can bring us closer together. Michael Easter underlines this point in his book *Scarcity Brain* when he writes, "We are not wired to enjoy things; we are wired to seek."

In the past, if we were lucky enough to come across a bunch of sugary fruit, the best plan was to eat as much as possible, because that opportunity might not come along again for a very long time. In a world where most people have enough food to eat, overeating is on the rise. Our brains evolved in a world where food security simply did not exist. This makes us crave high-calorie foods over low-calorie ones. Our bodies assume that the more calories food contains, the better it is. The more we eat, the more fat we store, and the more secure we feel moving forward. While this is a great strategy in a world with limited calories, our modern world looks increasingly like a setup for the obesity epidemic that is clearly underway. The reality is that we are wired not only to crave high-calorie foods but also to seek scarce resources in other areas of our lives. Why does this persist?

We have a scarcity mindset built into our brains. When we receive "scarcity cues," we do whatever it takes to feel whole.

43

Research on modern people shows that we use money to signal three distinct but overlapping messages to the world around us.

First, we use money and possessions to create the appearance of security. Modern people mix up the notion of security — *I have enough to survive* — with trust — *I have people in my life who will support me.* It is true that if I have enough resources, my family will be more secure. But in a world full of stuff that can be purchased, we mistake material abundance for community support.

The second thing is that money helps us signal our relative social status. There weren't many ways to distinguish ourselves from others when we all lived in small villages. Social status was important, but you couldn't separate yourself too much from those around you. All that has changed. We can purchase nicer cars, bigger houses, designer clothes, and countless other items to signal our social status to those around us. In our modern lives, this can get out of hand quickly.

Third, we are leading lives that are more isolated than our ancestors could have ever imagined. As we move to new cities, we turn our familial connections into long-distance relationships. Our daily interactions involve an incredible diversity of different people. We often spend hours in front of computer screens, sometimes in meetings but typically alone in a room. We have a relative level of security but lack the intimacy we require. Whereas our ancestors used money to increase security, we try to find a sense of belonging by purchasing more stuff, even though we are lonelier than ever before.

We use purchases to signify our cultural identity and to indicate our position in the social hierarchy. You want everyone to know that you eat at this restaurant, buy this designer, or shop in that store, and you do this to feel like you belong. Easter writes that "scientists now call this 'brand tribalism.' It's where we find social meaning from the purchases we make." It is exactly at this juncture that our modern lives have gone off the rails.

In his book *The Psychology of Money*, Morgan Housel writes

that the hardest financial skill to learn is to stop moving the goalposts: "Modern capitalism is a pro at two things: generating wealth and generating envy... but life isn't any fun without a sense of enough." We are wired to compare ourselves to one another, and because of this, we continuously adjust our standards. This drops us into the abundance-scarcity cycle that we are all trying to escape. We work more to make more because we want to feel like we belong.

Our ancient ancestors lived in relatively small, tight-knit villages. They already had intimacy and used money to buy security. Our lives are completely reversed. We generally have an abundance of scarce resources but lack deep, intimate connections. They had a sense of belonging, while we try to purchase intimacy by accumulating things.

We don't need to romanticize going back to the land or imitating our ancestors. Rather, we need to bring awareness to *why* we are still trying to accumulate more things, even though we have more than we can fit into our lives. We have mixed up buying rare items with embodying the meaningful moments we experience. If we want to be the kind of people others want to be around, we need to learn to integrate the more profound elements of our existence. This is what makes us unique and brings value to others.

Money is not a thing. It is a social technology used to create trust and credit — a belief in social reciprocity — with people outside our intimate social circles. We can't use money to convince people that we belong. Nor can we accumulate an abundance of stuff to convince others that we are trustworthy. To create intimacy, we need to be vulnerable. For someone to really trust you, they must know they can count on you in their most vulnerable moments. They need you to show up consistently during their greatest time of need. But because so many of our basic needs are met in the modern world, we have mistaken belongings for belonging.

Money cannot buy you intimacy, no matter how much of

it you have. After reaching a certain threshold — the level at which your basic needs are met and you feel secure — money cannot solve your problems. But it can help create opportunities for growth and purpose. It can allow us to create contexts to build strong social bonds. Money is a guide that is waiting for you to listen to what it has been trying to teach you all along. It is trying to point to areas where you feel a lack — not of stuff but of meaning.

• MINI MOMENT •

Where do I feel a sense of lack in my life?
What lesson is money trying to teach me?

What Makes You Truly Secure

There are aspects of our lives beyond security that create meaning. Intimacy is one of them, but we also need other experiences, such as vitality and growth, that money cannot buy. Together, they are part of the infinite game of life that requires a focus on quality over quantity. In the finite game of scarce resources, we can accumulate an abundance of stuff to create a sense of security. In the infinite game, we are after meaningful experiences. These cannot be amassed like money; they need to be digested and integrated.

One of the most common misnomers in the financial world is when we refer to investments as "securities." This implies that the more investments we have, the more secure we are. Or that the more money we acquire, the safer we will feel. While money plays a role in creating a solid foundation, it will only get us so far in addressing what is essentially a nonmonetary problem.

If we haven't found security, intimacy, and belonging within our awareness or nurtured a sense of being enough, we will inadvertently depend on money for reassurance or become overly focused on future financial goals. When we don't have the tools to cultivate security *as an innate experience*, we lean too heavily on the material world to provide it. We can stockpile all we want, but if we don't figure out how to be in relationship with our anxieties, worries, and fears, no amount of money will make the emotional turmoil go away. Money cannot replace our need for the support we receive from healthy relationships with other human beings and the natural world.

As humans, we are here to evolve. To expand our experience of wealth, we must broaden our vision of success and economics. No matter how many resources we accumulate, they will not bring us a lasting sense of being part of something larger than ourselves.

Being in charge is *our* role, not money's. We hold the power to define new wealth metrics. We can determine and design our own parameters for success. When we find the courage to question the limitations of our current financial system, starting with redefining and embracing a wider perspective of wealth, we restore the proper function of money as a social technology and currency of trust. Money, used in the proper way, helps us reclaim wealth as our birthright and as a conduit to well-being.

Chapter 2 Takeaways

Money as a Social Technology: Money facilitates relationships and trust beyond our intimate circles. It acts as a technology of relationships and a form of social credit, allowing us to gauge the trustworthiness and reliability of people we don't know well. Throughout history, money has taken various forms, from shell beads to digital currencies, demonstrating that its value is based on social agreements rather than intrinsic worth.

Money Can't Buy Intimacy: While money can help us achieve a sense of security by acquiring scarce resources, it cannot buy intimacy or a deep sense of belonging. Our modern lives often lack the close-knit communities our ancestors had, leading us to mistakenly seek belonging through accumulating possessions. However, true intimacy and trust are built through sharing vulnerabilities, consistent presence, and communal experiences.

Money Affords Opportunities for Meaning: Although money cannot buy growth and development, it can open doors to new opportunities, experiences, and forms of participation. Ultimately, wealth is a combination of having sufficient resources for security; intimate relationships that provide trust, purpose, and belonging; and the development that comes through a commitment to personal growth, which can create a sense of freedom and creativity. When put together, integrating and embodying experiences of abundance, intimacy, and growth brings meaning to our lives.

Chapter Three

CONVERSATIONS WITH MONEY

Stop Blaming Money, and Start Owning Your Life

What if I told you the most effective way to create more joy in your relationship with money is as straightforward as sitting down and having a conversation with it? You might feel a surge of curiosity, experience a mental blank, stifle an internal groan, or even close this book altogether and stop reading. I get it. I've been there. This chapter unveils one of the most provoking and powerful practices I teach — the art of engaging in a genuine conversation with money. More importantly, it delves into the crucial skill of not just speaking to money but truly listening to its response.

Let that sink in: Money has its own perspective and opinion on how you manage and connect with it. If you're looking for a surefire path to increased joy and ease with your finances, extend the same level of consideration and respect to your relationship with money that you do to any other meaningful relationship in your life.

As with any relationship, it's crucial to view our connection with money as a two-way street. Authentic rapport doesn't flourish in an environment where one party exerts unnecessary control, acts overbearingly, or becomes authoritarian. In fact, when this happens, we tend to walk away. Our relationship with money works best when we are in *dialogue* with it, remain adaptable, and heed its feedback on how we treat it, use it, earn it, and spend it. In this way, instead of defining us, money can become a trusted advisor and friend.

Are you unfairly blaming money for your behavior instead of taking responsibility for it? Are you using the lack of money as a scapegoat for your own shortcomings when it could be that you might lack essential qualities like courage and grit for your own transformation? Or are you conflating your relationship with money with another challenging relationship in your life? During times of distress, do you manipulate or withhold money as a form of punishment? The list goes on, and in some form or another, we have all participated.

We often misuse money to vent frustrations and as a pretext to avoid taking certain risks that can lead to more fulfillment in our lives. The practice outlined in this chapter is designed to help you make use of money differently, distinguishing between what pertains to money and what does not. Through this discernment, you'll attain a clearer understanding of the barriers preventing you from experiencing joy, not just in your relationship with money but also in your broader life. This is how we unravel the connection between money and our self-worth.

The notion of sitting down and having a conversation with money (or CW$ for short) might seem unconventional. Yet when embraced, something mysterious and magical occurs. This practice has the power to cut through layers of hurt and confusion, enabling you to set aside the aspects of money that remain elusive and connect with what you authentically feel.

These feelings may not always be pleasant or positive, but expressing them provides an opportunity to delve beneath the narratives you've woven about yourself and money — whether they're about your proficiency and knowledge in handling it or your lack thereof. By doing so, you can touch the potential within you to establish a more harmonious relationship with money. A CW$

gives you an opportunity to digest this relationship, allowing you to integrate what serves you and let go of what doesn't.

Here's a truth I share with all my clients: I can serve as an expert who helps design and implement financial strategies, but I cannot stand in for their personal relationship with money. No one can.

> • MINI MOMENT •
>
> Do I feel I have a direct relationship with money? Or is there someone or something else standing in the way?

A CW$ takes you to the heart of the matter, placing you in unfiltered, direct contact with your financial reality. The power of this exchange lies in its ability to pinpoint what's functioning well in your financial realm, and more crucially, what's not. It starts with a simple act: talking to money and genuinely listening to what it has to say in response.

Ultimately, it doesn't matter whether you believe you're truly speaking with money. What's important is recognizing that there is a part of you that grapples with financial matters almost daily, and perhaps that part has insights to share.

A CW$ is not always easy. When I ask people, "What would you say if you had the chance to talk to money?" I get a range of reactions. Many burst into nervous laughter; some resort to cracking jokes; others find themselves at a loss for words. Then follows a moment of uneasy silence, typically accompanied by some form of resistance and a variation of "Do I really have to answer that?"

The truth is that most of us are inclined to scapegoat money. It seems too abstract and elusive, never quite manifesting in the way or amount we desire, or slipping away before we can grasp it. Even when we earn and have an abundance of it, the desire for more often lingers.

I wholeheartedly acknowledge the complexity of our monetary and financial systems, which we dove into in chapter 2. In fact, I spend many hours in client conversations every day trying to simplify money. However, part of our personal maturity is recognizing that we don't need to fully understand every aspect of something before finding more effective ways to relate to it.

Engaging in a CW$ is a transformative practice aimed at wiping the slate clean and constructing a relationship grounded in mutual respect, trust, and collaboration. If your aim is to infuse more joy into your interactions with money, start by casting aside excuses and identifying the obstacles that hinder your ability to experience greater ease and delight with it. Yes, I did say delight.

Emotions Are a Priceless Resource

Later in the book, we will talk about how our stories about money wield significant power. When we keep our money stories cloaked in secrecy, we are not able to digest and integrate them. When ignored and pushed away, these stories occupy too much mental space. We can think of money as a guide or teacher that has an important lesson about life for us to learn. When we push money away, the lesson goes unlearned, and we find ourselves repeating unhelpful patterns because we have not taken the time to listen to what money is trying to say.

The more we open and share, the more we learn, the more we can digest and integrate the lessons money has given us. Exploring financial mistakes and successes enables us to view them with less gravity. As we engage in dialogue with money, we move toward growth and increase meaning in our lives. And with each CW$, you might start to realize that money is on your side.

There is an important shift here where you come to realize that money is not actively obstructing your dreams, but rather challenging you to step into new opportunities for growth and meaning. The point of your relationship with money shifts from attempting to accumulate abundance and ensure security to something far more exciting. Money becomes a partner, friend, and mentor, helping you fully engage in the adventure that is your life.

Money can help us move toward something deeper, but we fail to do this due to the unresolved currents of scarcity in our lives. Instead of listening to money, we try to accumulate resources to create a sense of abundance. But this only goes so far. Accumulating stuff only works to solve our need for security. Life has everything to do with growth and meaning. To take steps on this journey, we need to digest our unresolved thoughts and emotions that keep us trapped in the abundance-scarcity cycle.

The lessons we learn through our CW$ are relatively simple but hard to integrate. Our unresolved thoughts and emotions hold vital information — they are like golden nuggets of wisdom, rich with insight, creativity, passion, and an array of elements that contribute to a more present and grounded existence. Maintaining a healthy relationship with our thoughts and emotions is integral to feeling complete and whole. This is money's gift to us, shifting our attention from abundance and scarcity to vitality and intimacy.

This might sound counterintuitive at first. How does expressing our hurt or anger at money contribute to creating more joy? Opportunities for growth and development lie in recognizing that concealing or ignoring our feelings about money yields a negative return on our investment of time and energy. Suppressing emotions requires effort and attention, occupying mental and emotional space that could be better directed toward creating joy.

Emotions are rapid, reflexive responses to external stimuli. In less than ninety seconds, the chemistry of an emotion floods through our body and courses in our bloodstream. At a fundamental level, we may never outgrow our feelings of anger and resentment, but we can evolve our expression and utilization of these emotional responses.

Whether consciously or unconsciously, when emotions surface, a choice emerges. We can opt to ignore the thoughts and experiences that triggered the emotion, prolonging the experience of that emotional state. Or we can acknowledge that emotions have their natural course and instead choose to dwell in the space where understanding emerges. Emotions are potent bundles of energy, and energy is a priceless economic resource. When we digest and integrate the energy of emotions, we can transform any feeling into the energy of insight and metamorphosis. A heightened connection to this resource establishes a stronger foundation for the creation of wealth based not only on accumulating an abundance of scarce resources but also on accumulating growth and meaning in our lives.

> • MINI MOMENT •
>
> What's my primary emotional connection to money?

Familiarity with Money Is Key

In her groundbreaking book *Whole Brain Living*, Jill Bolte Taylor unravels the intricate workings of our brains' emotional processing. As external stimuli filter through our sensory systems, our amygdala serves as the initial checkpoint by asking, Is this situation safe? Our sense of safety hinges on how familiar we are with what we're engaging with.

When faced with the unknown, the amygdala tends to label the experience as a potential threat, triggering our fight, flight, or freeze response. To move forward and transform, we must consciously pause and allow these challenging responses to course through our body. As part of this process, we must opt to digest the experience by integrating what serves us and eliminating what needs to go, rather than opting to ignore it and thereby stay in the thought pattern that continues to restimulate the story. As we listen to money and lean into our more challenging patterns of thought and emotion, we can lift the fog hindering our ability to think clearly when it comes to money and financial decisions.

This underscores the role of a CW$ as a potent tool and technique. Not only does it allow us to release pent-up emotions and learn from the stories we associate with money, but it also fosters a deeper sense of familiarity with money over time. This is key. Having a genuine familiarity or closeness with money can be an important deterrent against the inclination to amass more resources for a false sense of security. When we are familiar with something, we are more likely to trust its guidance and presence in our life.

The way to leverage our thoughts and emotions into energy is to create more productive responses to our established financial patterns and habits. If you're harboring irritation or anger toward money but refrain from expressing it, that unresolved emotion becomes a corrosive force, potentially driving hasty and impulsive financial decisions. I've witnessed firsthand how clients, fueled by fury toward someone else, impulsively charge an unplanned purchase to their credit card, especially if the other person was responsible for paying the bill. But this doesn't solve the problem. Rather, the act of expressing and confronting these emotions is an essential step toward financial well-being.

Similarly, if you find yourself overwhelmed by financial concerns, you might miss taking creative or professional risks. Or feeling depressed about what you have or don't have can cloud your ability to recognize opportunities in unexpected places. Engaging in a CW$ can unveil the true source of your anger, anxiety, or distress. Often, you'll discover that your thoughts and emotions are not directly tied to money itself but stem from an unresolved experience with someone or something else. Making these distinctions between what truly pertains to money and what does not is a crucial step in unlocking more growth and meaning in your financial life.

• MINI MOMENT •

What words currently describe my emotions and relationship with money?

Words matter. Naming an emotion helps us navigate from an emotional state to a thinking state where we can work with the energy instead of being consumed by it.

A CW$ is essentially a creative take on the well-known Gestalt empty chair therapeutic exercise. In this practice, you place money or a symbolic representation of it in an empty chair in front of you. You then express your feelings toward it freely. After you share, the focus turns to money, allowing it a chance to respond. The aim? To create a cathartic dialogue between you and your money.

I learned this method from the psychologist Michael Klein during my master's program at the California Institute of Integral Studies (CIIS). In the middle of a weekend workshop, he dropped a powerful truth: "If you don't confront your relationship with money head-on, success with it will elude you." The room fell silent. In our transpersonal psychology cohort at CIIS, dealing with the day-to-day aspects of money was unfamiliar terrain.

Dr. Klein's statement lingered heavily in the air. The idea of directly addressing our relationship with money felt nearly impossible, like attempting to embrace a shadow that consistently slipped through our grasp.

He persisted, unfazed, emphasizing that the most significant task in our future careers was to approach money with the same consideration and respect we would show a family member. We paired up to take turns having conversations with money. It all sounded straightforward and easy. Yet letting go of my preconceived notions of money and speaking my unfiltered truth was more challenging than I could have ever imagined.

Holding On to Money Too Tightly

My first CW$ revealed a deep-seated resentment and anger toward money, stemming from the pressure to figure out how to earn it, set client fees, and navigate its role in my life.

When I sat down to begin, I immediately felt resistance. There was no part of me that wanted to admit in front of a stranger just how much I struggled with money. I already felt like an impostor, and I was now being asked to say all that out loud.

I righteously told money I was extremely mad at it for not showing up in my life. I was angry about its perceived absence and frustrated by the lack of clarity on how to build my practice and define my client offerings. The urgency to secure additional funds to launch my business intensified, and impatience gripped me. Ugh! I was so irritated at money. I loathed its intangibility and how, despite my efforts, it constantly slipped through my fingers. I continued to vent, allowing the waves of frustration to subside only when I felt a sense of completion.

Then came the interesting part. The narrative took a riveting turn as my partner tactfully signaled it was time to change chairs. Reluctantly, I shifted into the seat directly before me, now speaking as money. Clutching my chosen object — a credit card burdened with an outstanding balance I was diligently trying to pay off — I held money on my lap. I closed my eyes and took a moment to assume my new role.

Here is what money said:

Elizabeth, you hold on way too tightly. You strangle me and control me. You want me to be there, but then you don't go out and find me, so you cling to what is given to you.

You've never really tried to make me. I've always come your way through others, like your dad. You're scared that if that source dries up, you won't have more of me.

57

Don't put your fear on me. That is not mine to hold.
If you grow up and start your business earnestly, we will
be able to engage in a whole different way. Own your fear.
Find support to work through it. I'll meet you halfway.

A wave of shock swept over me. Money challenged my sense
of entitlement and urged me to confront my fears. It astutely
pointed out that my struggle to generate income was not its fault,
nor mine for that matter. Instead, it recognized that I was *choosing*
to engage with a new professional reality, and that what I needed
was more guidance on how to succeed.

Ironically, money expressed a belief in my capacity to learn how
to become an entrepreneur, but it would not serve our relationship
if I suffocated it in the process. In fact, the unspoken warning was
clear: Shed this behavior to strengthen our partnership. The responsibility for acquiring the necessary skills for business development
lay squarely on my shoulders. By scapegoating money, I unwittingly
squandered my precious time, energy, and resources.

Following my heart-to-heart with money, I realized that I had
the power to redefine my relationship with earnings. It was no
longer a battle of me versus money. Money was more of a cheer-
leader, rooting for my success. This shift from distrust to cama-
raderie opened the door to a fresh alliance based on trust and
common aspirations.

After my first CW$ session, I raised my client rates and fine-
tuned my services; four years down the road, I joined a financial
planning firm. Instead of holding on to resentment, I focused on
pinpointing my areas of ignorance and seeking the necessary support. Surprisingly, money evolved into a crucial element of my
support network. I made it a daily ritual, using it as a sounding
board for ideas and a compass for navigating new directions.

A CW$ is a blueprint for honest money talk. It is a power-
house tool that sparks deep healing when we muster the courage
to face our feelings about money directly.

Money Is Not Good or Evil

Let's reexamine an important myth: Money isn't inherently good or evil. People often assign these moral qualities to money. In reality, it is neither.

While it's true that we can misuse money to cause harm, seeing money only through a negative lens conceals an essential truth: Money is merely one of the many tools humans use to navigate the world. By acknowledging this, we stop blaming money and begin digging into the juicy stuff — our insecurities, power-hungry habits, and never-ending appetite for more. This is where the real work lies.

Taking responsibility for your action or inaction with money is a potent step toward reclaiming your power. Expressing pent-up emotions, working through your money stories, admitting your shortcomings, and seeking help when needed can bring a deeper sense of coherence to your life. Your relationship to money and the emotions you associate with it is another entry point into knowing who you truly are.

Your first attempt at a CW$ might feel like an exploration of therapy-related territory, presenting a multitude of challenges. Whether you are quick to spill your emotions or struggle to find the right words, the first dive can be daunting. Having a supportive companion holding space made a world of difference for me. So if you decide to take the plunge and encounter radio silence, keep these considerations close at hand.

From my experience of coaching countless individuals through their initial CW$, one undeniable truth emerges: everyone, regardless of financial standing, carries baggage related to money and stands to benefit from engaging with those emotions. Recognizing this shared human experience is liberating. Realizing that you are not alone in your conflict with money is an important starting point.

What if the goal were no longer amassing wealth to the point of not having to even *think* about money anymore? Instead, the vision would be to have a healthy and vibrant relationship *with* money where you felt confident in your ability to face any life situation head-on. Success is not a onetime occurrence measured by accolades or amassed wealth. Real success unfolds over time, more like a habit than a singular moment in your life story. It is the realization that you possess the resilience and capabilities — including tools like CW$ — to confront any challenges life presents. Let's dive in.

PRACTICE: Your First Conversation with Money (CW$)

Step 1: Choose Your Money Object

First things first — this practice starts with the exercise of choosing something that represents money for you. Take a moment to reflect on the various forms of money that are intertwined in your daily life. It could be the tangible — bills, change, your wallet, a credit card, a checkbook, your smartphone — or something abstract — a family heirloom, a piece of jewelry, an antique coin. Get creative. Allow yourself to be surprised as you look for something that symbolizes money to you.

In a particularly memorable CW$ session, a client chose to work with a piece of gold. This wasn't just any gold — it was a gift from his hardworking assayer mom, who once braved the mines of Nevada. The gold piece carried the weight of her toil and sacrifice. Even though his family's mining hardships were in the past, the client wanted to tackle lingering beliefs that making money was an uphill battle. The piece of gold became the perfect conduit for this exploration.

If you find yourself torn between various options, ask yourself these guiding questions:

1. Which of these money objects sparks joy and a sense of ease?
2. Or, on the other hand, which money object triggers aversion or tension?

Whether it's saying a simple hello to money or delving into deeper conversations, your chosen money object serves as a powerful catalyst to explore whatever money emotion or behavior feels most important to you.

Some people are prepared to confront the core issue directly, opting for an object that embodies the friction, anxiety, or stress associated with money. Others want an easier introduction and choose something that reminds them what they like about money.

If you grapple with debt, consider initiating a conversation with your credit card. If you tend to overspend, a wallet might be a fitting choice. If you obsess about money, your smartphone — always at your fingertips for financial monitoring — might serve as a potent tool. There's no perfect money object for this practice; what matters most is selecting something that inspires you to engage with money, even if the emotions tied to it are uncomfortable. The true power of this practice emerges when you allow yourself to be surprised by what unfolds in the dialogue and embrace the unexpected revelations that clamor to be expressed.

Step 2: Create the Container

Once you have picked your money object, it's time to elevate the experience by giving it a stage. Create a container for your CW$. Think of how you would prepare if you invited a close friend over for a cup of tea. Designate a special spot, a money haven if you will, where both you and money can feel the love and security. This intentional act contributes to the depth and authenticity of the conversation and fosters a conducive space for open expression and mutual understanding.

1. Choose the location and type of chairs that resonate for you. Whether it's literal chairs, designated spots on a couch, or meditation pillows on the floor, infuse intention into this choice. Recognize that your chosen space is the bedrock of a safe environment uniquely crafted and curated by you.

2. Deliberately decide the proximity of your seat and money's seat. If you grapple with tendencies like hoarding or controlling money, consider placing it slightly farther away to create more energetic space between the two of you. Alternatively, if trust is a challenge, consider bringing the chairs closer together to foster intimacy and goodwill. This is a dynamic step. You can adjust the distance between you and money at any point in the conversation.

3. Once both you and money are comfortably situated, close your eyes and take one full-body breath. Channel your awareness toward whatever emotion or feeling is there. Greet it with a simple hello, acknowledging its presence. This foundational breath sets the tone for an open and authentic exchange, establishing a space where emotions can be explored and expressed.

Step 3: You Get to Go First

Once you've settled into your body, extend the moment of having your eyes closed and envision a distinct knocking sound at the door. *Knock, knock, knock!* Money has arrived, ready to take a seat in front of you.

Open your eyes, addressing money in the first person

using "I" statements. Envision money as a living entity, vividly present right before you. Take a moment to gather the nuances of your experience. What are your genuine feelings about money? What needs to be expressed to kick-start an honest conversation?

Maintain eye contact with money as you speak, allowing your words to flow without the hindrance of self-editing or interruption. Resist the inclination to recount your entire money story; save that for the separate practice detailed in chapter 9. Money has been a silent companion throughout those moments. Now it craves your unfiltered, honest emotions. The more you stay connected to your feelings and express them authentically in a first-person dialogue, the more liberating the experience becomes.

Keep the conversation going for as long as you need. Allow the momentum to build naturally; when it starts to slow down, pause and take another full-body breath. Acknowledge the courage and vulnerability it took to unload those emotions.

Step 4: Money Responds

When you are done speaking to money, switch chairs and let money have a turn. This means literally moving physically, taking money's seat and holding your money object in your lap. Allow yourself a moment to settle into this new perspective. Glance back at the chair you just vacated — it now symbolizes you. Now you assume the role of money, providing it an opportunity to respond and articulate its perspective.

Allow yourself to be both curious and surprised as money speaks through you, responding to what you have expressed. Whether offering clarifications, providing honest feedback, or posing questions, embrace the same guiding principles.

Ensure that money is kind, yet unreservedly honest. This is money's chance to express its authentic viewpoint.

Take all the time you need to articulate the response as money. When you sense the conversation naturally ending, pause and allow some time for everything that has been said to integrate. You might find yourself pleasantly surprised by the revelations that money imparts and the ease with which it communicates its insights.

Step 5: Dialogue as Currency, a Fluid Back-and-Forth

Following money's initial response, it's important to keep the conversation open. Feel free to switch positions again and resume the dialogue from your original seat. It is like a conversation dance, going back and forth until you feel complete.

If you opt for another turn, extend the same courtesy to money. Ensure both perspectives have an equal opportunity to express themselves, even if it means sitting in silence until another round of unspoken thoughts emerges.

Step 6: Express Gratitude

When both you and money feel complete, end the conversation from one of the roles. Find some way to express gratitude, either through words or a gesture, especially if the exchange was challenging and emotionally charged. This can be a gentle bow of the head, an act of bringing your hands to your heart, or a straightforward thank-you. Regardless of how you choose to end the conversation, infuse it with deliberate intention to bring closure to the practice.

Honor yourself for having the courage to do this in the first place. Appreciate money for its participation. A CW$ is a new practice that requires flexing a different muscle. Be gentle with yourself. Be gracious with money. And like always, be surprised at what can arise.

Step 7: End with Satiation

The last step for this practice is to return to your starting point by gently closing your eyes. Let go of your money object. Redirect your awareness back to your breath, but this time, incorporate an awareness of your ability to swallow. This movement enables us to *consume* nourishment — to nourish yourself with your own insights and awareness.

Focus on a key insight gleaned from the practice, be it a realization you gained yourself or a reflection offered by money. As you swallow, allow this insight to permeate within the deepest cells of your body, extending all the way down to your toes. Feel the embodiment of a renewed relationship with money, noting the subtle shifts and observing how your body incorporates this newfound awareness. As we discussed in chapter 1, integration becomes the foundational framework for creating reference points in your journey to embody wealth.

Open your eyes only when you feel ready. Gradually return to your surroundings. Acknowledge that the practice has concluded, leaving you with new insights, heightened awareness, and a transformational practice to engage with.

Helpful Guidelines

- **EMBRACE RESISTANCE:** Nine out of ten clients engaging in this exercise initially report feelings of resistance. If you sense resistance, recognize it as a guardian of your hidden treasures and totally normal. Embrace resistance as a guardian of insights and lower your shields to let them surface.

- **USE A TIMER:** Speaking about money can be challenging, and maintaining the duration of a CW$ requires discipline. Consider using a timer to add structure. Allocate three minutes for each turn; when the timer sounds, switch roles and set it again for the same amount of time. Repeat each role at least twice using the timer for added consistency.

- **AVOID SELF-EDITING:** Resist the urge to edit yourself or hinder the process. This is an opportunity for unfiltered honesty about your feelings regarding money. Approach it as a judgment-free practice, giving yourself permission to express yourself in any manner necessary. Utilize strong words, metaphors, and gestures — let it all out. Seize the present moment to unburden yourself.

- **STAY FOCUSED:** Avoid getting lost in your money story; this exercise is about expressing emotions, not recounting your financial history. Stick to the emotions you feel about money and communicate directly with those sentiments. Money knows your story quite intimately; this is about acknowledging your emotional connection to it.

- **ASK FOR SUPPORT AND WITNESSING:** If the process feels too challenging to do on your own, seek support. Or if nothing happens, seek support. Bring the practice to your therapist, or ask a trusted friend or partner to witness the dialogue. Their role is not to intervene but to provide support and prompt with questions if needed. As highlighted in my first CW$, sometimes the act of having someone else there goes a long way in getting the conversation going.

- **WHAT IF IT GETS UGLY?** I suggest three things:
  1. Pause and allow intense emotions to surface. Take deep breaths, let feelings emerge, and use movement to release tension.
  2. Say what is relevant but stay kind. Avoid self-harm. If overwhelmed, seek assistance. Speaking with brutal honesty, coupled with kindness, maintains presence and openness.
  3. If you start to shut down, stop the exercise entirely. Identify activated boundaries and gain clarity. Awareness alone can be a starting point.

- **WHAT IF NOTHING HAPPENS?** If nothing seems to happen when you start your CW$, or if engaging in a spoken dialogue with money feels too abstract or challenging, adapt this practice into a writing exercise. Grab your journal and use the same prompts outlined above. Instead of verbal interaction, express your feelings through writing. When it's money's turn, draw a line beneath your written thoughts and allow money to write. This modification ensures flexibility in the practice, catering to different preferences and comfort levels. Writing provides a tangible outlet for your emotions, offering an alternative yet equally powerful means of exploring your relationship with money.

- **WRITE YOUR INSIGHTS DOWN:** There is no right or wrong way to do this practice. Let the dialogue be fluid, dynamic, vital, and even intense. It might be helpful to document some of your insights from the practice. Consider prompts such as the following:
  ‣ What was your main takeaway?
  ‣ How did it feel to voice your feelings about money?

- What surprised you during money's response?
- Was there a clear action step identified for both you and money to deepen your relationship?

Your first CW$ might be the hardest. Most of us will feel awkward, strange, and a little disoriented at even the thought of talking to money, much less doing it. Yet, over time, this simple practice might become one of your most potent money tools. It offers a direct and clear pathway to delve into the core of any financial matter you encounter.

I strongly encourage you to find a way to make this a regular practice. With time, it becomes more manageable and even something to anticipate.

One of my morning rituals involves a cup of yerba maté tea, which takes about ten minutes to steep. For years, I incorporated a morning CW$ while waiting for my tea. Seated on meditation pillows, with my money jar on one of them, I engaged in a daily CW$. Using a two-minute timer for each role, I stopped my practice after eight minutes and recorded insights in my journal while I sipped my tea. Over time, money and I developed a fluid conversation, transforming money from a source of contention into a trusted friend.

Make this practice your own. Adapt it to suit your rhythm, space, and pace. Whether it becomes casual talk on the couch or conversations during workouts at the gym is inconsequential. A CW$ can happen anywhere, anytime. Find your groove with CW$ that aligns with your preferences. Adjust the tempo when needed, take plenty of breaks, and regularly come back to the metaphorical cushion to speak with money, building a deep-seated and trusting relationship with it.

Chapter 3 Takeaways

A Conversation with Money: A CW$ is not a conversation about money, but rather one *with* money. Sit down and talk to it. Open yourself to hearing what money has to offer in return.

Initiate a Real Relationship: Many of us have never established a genuine relationship with money, and that's perfectly acceptable. The key is to start now. Recognize that a relationship with money is reciprocal. As you take responsibility for your behaviors that shape your financial reality, and cease blaming money, you move toward greater financial freedom and interdependence. Face fears, embrace insecurities, seek help, and initiate the dialogue with money to understand its perspective.

Build the CW$ Muscle: Treat the CW$ practice as a muscle that needs strengthening and consistent development. Understand that one CW$ session won't miraculously solve all your financial challenges. Instead, commit to a regular practice, viewing it as a long-term commitment that has the potential to bring about positive changes over time.

Chapter Four

DIALOGUE AS CURRENCY

What You and Money Are Meant to Achieve

Time and time again, I've seen significant and transformative changes emerge when people courageously sit down and have a conversation with money. While similar themes and patterns are present, each exchange is unique.

In this chapter, I share two client stories that offer a perspective through which you may resonate or find reflections of your own. The narratives highlight that money is a social technology meant to be used. These conversations offer new angles on what it means to be in relationship with money, and that dialogue is valuable currency. Currency serves as a means of exchange. Our words with money offer a similar convenience that has been overlooked.

When we step into a conversation with purpose, ready to listen and open to feedback, magic happens, allowing a real exchange to occur. Authentic dialogue supports us in developing a growth mindset. Both sides walk away richer — not in dollars but in awareness and insight, creating a different form of wealth: deeper fulfillment.

A key habit for cultivating a growth mindset is "thinking win-win." It's not about being nice or finding a shortcut. It is a character-based code for how people interact and collaborate, and it can transform how we approach relationships. If we perceive life as a zero-sum game, someone must lose for another to win. But if we adopt a collaborative worldview, we seek mutual benefit for all involved, even if it means adjusting our initial expectations.

This profound shift in perspective not only fosters lasting, positive connections but also highlights that experiencing more wealth, in the broader sense, doesn't diminish others' ability to experience wealth at the same time. In fact, understanding and amplifying what creates wealth for you can inspire others in unexpected ways. A collaborative relationship with money creates a win-win scenario. Money is attracted to ideas in motion, and it wants to flow. You just need to sit down, talk with it, and be clear on how each of you needs to show up differently to make it work.

In the case of these two clients, the CW$ became an ongoing practice that made important "deposits" in their social, emotional, and mental bank accounts. These deposits created a new foundation on which to build wealth and cultivate a greater sense of teamwork with money.

More Money Does Not Solve Everything

At a relatively young age, Jonathan had amassed substantial wealth through the sale of his company. This remarkable accomplishment meant he was financially independent. Given his assets and lifestyle, he no longer needed to work. While impressive, such financial independence in a short period of time also brought challenges.

Jonathan initially sought my expertise in behavioral finance, not financial planning. He acknowledged that despite his considerable wealth, he opted to keep most of it in cash, driven by an overpowering fear of potential losses. This seemingly irrational choice became the focal point of our work together. At the age of thirty-three, Jonathan recognized that he needed some growth in his funds to guard against inflation. Nevertheless, Jonathan felt apprehensive about investing when he felt so conflicted about money to begin with.

We discovered that it wasn't a fundamental aversion to risk that held him back; after all, he had amassed his wealth as an entrepreneur, a venture inherently filled with risk. Rather, the nuanced motivation behind his irrational dislike for having his money make more money stemmed from unresolved anger toward his father.

Jonathan described his father as an extreme hoarder and obsessive worker. He vividly recalled his father fixated on accumulating more wealth and savings. This relentless pursuit of financial security came at a price. His father was absent in pivotal family moments, many of which Jonathan recounted with hurt and anger. Unknowingly, his father deprived his children of the chance to create intimacy and share in the simple joy of reveling in each other's presence as an *experience* of having and being enough.

In Jonathan's family narrative, the stark emphasis on accumulating "financial bonds" over "familial bonds" served as a powerful metaphor. His father's focus on financial security and tangible assets rather than intangible familial connections had a lasting impact on Jonathan's relationship with money. Money had become a stand-in and a scapegoat for unresolved issues in his family. He was determined not to repeat the same mistakes.

• MINI MOMENT •

Who in my life overemphasized money to the detriment of our relationship? How did it feel?

The research here is clear: Beyond a certain threshold of accumulated wealth, the pursuit of more money does not necessarily enhance happiness. In fact, the opposite can occur. The desire for more and more money becomes detrimental when it overtakes other aspects that are just as crucial for our well-being.

Economists call this the law of diminishing returns — benefits gained become proportionally smaller as more money and energy are invested in the activity at hand. This is what makes scarcity so tricky. Our desires don't change; instead, they can exponentially grow as we become exposed to different lifestyles and abundant options. But the more choices we have, the harder it becomes to filter these choices through the lens of our authentic self and figure out what truly satiates us. The chatter of our monkey mind becomes incessant and the cost of each decision increases. We spend more time evaluating options and weighing optimal outcomes, at the expense of experiencing life. Jonathan was defying the advice of most financial planners he met with by keeping his assets in cash. But he knew he needed to get to the root of his disillusionment with money before generating more of it.

For Jonathan, the thought of creating more money only heightened his anxiety. It increased his sense of responsibility and intensified his fear that he would be further removed from what brought him joy. It became a vicious cycle with no apparent end. This mirrored what he saw in his father. While Jonathan's dad built financial wealth, it didn't lead to enhanced family connections or security.

From Scared to Sacred

At the start of Jonathan's first CW$, he was even-keeled about it. His first words were "Hey, money. Thank you for being a tool that grants me freedom. I appreciate that." It was as if we were talking to a coworker who had just done him a favor. He expressed gratitude and acknowledged money for being an instrument that afforded him many things.

As the CW$ unfolded, a subtle aversion started to surface.

His next words were "Money, I see how other people use you in bizarre ways. I feel like I've made a conscious choice to use you for good, but not everyone else has. You are a brilliant tool, but you can also be used to separate and divide. I see how humans get obsessed and blinded by you."

Jonathan resented money's power to influence people and engage them in a relentless game of comparison: "I hated who my dad became around you. My dad was too afraid of losing you and wanted to accumulate more. As a result, I never saw him. You were a vector for him, blinding him so much he never truly saw me. And that sucked."

Jonathan paused. He took a deep breath, opened his eyes, switched chairs, and asked money to chime in. Money's response went like this:

> Hi, Jonathan. You need to know I am just a construct. I am a tool created by humans to assign value. I'm here, just doing my thing.
>
> I'm sorry to hear about how you feel I affect humans, especially your dad. But the truth is, a lot of people aren't clear on how to use me properly.
>
> You need to get out of your head. Stop obsessing about losing me or feeling guilty about having me in the first place. Even better, stop avoiding me out of fear. You do not have to follow in your father's footsteps. You have the power to stop your own cycle of self-loathing and self-doubt.

I urged money to dive deeper and offer any advice on how Jonathan could break free from his own constraints. Money responded:

> Jonathan, I appreciate your openness to sit down and talk with me, but we need to establish better communication, mutual trust, and a clear plan.

75

Know where to use me and where not to. Know where I can strengthen connections and, more importantly, where I can't.

Don't hide behind me because you are unsure on how to have healthy and intimate relationships. I can be a partner and be used to get you the support you need.

Without these boundaries or support, you find yourself vacillating between spending me with guilt or clinging to me with fear. Ironically, this is when you become your father.

You feel overwhelmed right now because you don't have a job or structure. There is no clear next career step, partner, or home base. Choose what will most help you create a new sense of grounding, and let's work together to make it happen. I am not in your way; you are.

This was the emotional jackpot. Money was pointing out that despite his years of dedicated effort into building a successful company, he had unintentionally followed in his father's footsteps by accumulating financial wealth at the expense of his health and relationships. He ended up resembling his father more closely than he was willing to admit.

Jonathan could either continue to scapegoat money for his feelings of inadequacy and emptiness or take responsibility and gain clarity on what kept him from achieving embodied wealth. Talking with money unveiled a crucial truth — it couldn't fulfill or replace his need for meaningful connection, either with himself or with another person. Money was important, but it couldn't foster genuine, fulfilling connections in Jonathan's life.

Eventually, we all encounter financial patterns from our past. The choice is either to square our shoulders and confront directly what money has to say or to sweep it under the rug. By now, you know what path I would recommend. Our relationship to money is just another mirror to know ourselves. It is a journey toward self-awareness and transformation, and patterns that surface and are dealt with in this relationship will help you and others.

In subsequent sessions, it became evident that his deep feeling of inadequacy did not stem from his relationship with money, but rather from the belief that he was unable to establish a family that could truly experience genuine harmony and closeness. As he peeled back these layers, Jonathan unearthed his true longing — to have a life enriched by authentic connection, affection, and caring. He had transformed his relationship with money from *scared* to *sacred*.

Cultivating a healthy relationship with money is a deeply personal journey. While there might be shared concepts and strategies that can be universally applied, the essence of what you and money are meant to achieve — expressing your most genuine self in the material world — is inherently unique. Money can serve as a dynamic canvas, reflecting the rich diversity of individual experiences and aspirations that only you bring. I encourage you to engage with CW$ as a portal where the material and the sacred meet.

• MINI MOMENT •

What pattern, if shifted, would have the biggest impact on my relationship to money?

Money, I Am So Angry at You!

Another one of the more poignant CW$ I had the privilege of witnessing was with a woman named Cate, the proud owner of a landscaping business in the San Francisco Bay Area. Cate loved having her hands deep in rich soil. She had built a strong business crafting artful landscapes for a loyal clientele. Yet despite these achievements, financial wealth remained elusive.

In our sessions together, we delved into what money represented for Cate, uncovering a myriad of insights. What caught my attention was the profound anger that Cate harbored toward money. When presented with the opportunity to vent and confront money directly, she seized it with raw and unrestrained intensity:

> Money, I am so angry at you! I desperately want to believe that if I worked relentlessly, you'd just be there. I feel completely let down and betrayed.
>
> You are an arrogant son of a bitch. You come and go as you please. I feel like you test me and wait until the last second to show up. It's like you want to prove I will fail.
>
> You show up for people who just want to get more of you. They don't care about the world. They don't care about their friends. They don't care about service. I've tried to follow the meaningful path following the work I love, and not just wanting more of you.
>
> Frankly, I don't think you give a damn about me. I sweat over every single penny I get. You've never just fallen into my lap.

Cate paused and took a breath. She seemed startled by this display of anger. But there was a noticeable release, as if a weight had been lifted from her shoulders. She continued:

> You, after my family, are the primary source of anxiety in my life. I know that if there were a lot of you in my life, I would be doing great things.
>
> But the haunting belief persists — I am not good enough. I am unworthy of having you. It seems like only dishonest people get to have you. What good are you in this world anyway? You align yourself with those who are wicked. Sometimes I think the world would be better off

without you. You certainly do not deserve to consume this much energy in my life.

I then gently invited her to switch roles and ask money what it had to share in response:

Cate, you don't understand me at all, which makes it really challenging to want to talk to you. I feel unfairly blamed for all of humanity's flaws. I am not the root cause of human greed; those vices existed long before people started using me.

Greed and hatred persist even in the absence of money — they are rooted in emotions, psychological issues, and human breakdowns. Assigning the entirety of human pathology to me is unjust. I am just a piece of paper, essentially meaningless.

There was a moment of silence before money continued:

I don't want to engage with Cate. If someone is so blinded by their problems, getting too involved will result in only being blamed.

I say this with kindness — I don't deserve to be the sole focus of her issues. I thrive on making things happen. I appreciate all her ideas, but she sees herself as powerless. That's not my fault. Most of her issues arise from feelings of unworthiness, not me. She's trapped behind a glass wall. But if she were to take a closer look, the door to her freedom is wide open.

Her fears aren't about me; they're about whether she believes she's worthy enough to ask for me. She needs to own that.

Money responded with a fascinating mixture of exasperation and impatience, bluntly pushing Cate to take responsibility for her feelings of being undeserving. The crux of the matter was for Cate to recognize the value of her own work, charge fees that reflected this value, and confront the fear that not all clients would readily accept higher rates.

I gently prompted money for any further advice it had to offer:

Cate, against all odds, it's a miracle how far you've come. You've never really been taught how to manage me. I get that and I am sorry for that, but it is not my fault. Let's work together. Having this conversation is a crucial first step.

Let go of your money past. Ask for more of me from your clients. Shake off any noes and remember, if a client doesn't want to pay you for your work, you are creating more space for someone who does. Rally all the support you can to cultivate stronger roots of worthiness within yourself. Start there.

Cate was quiet for a long moment. Then, surprisingly, she brought her hands up to her heart center and did a gentle bow. It was almost as if after this CW$ she had no more words left.

I let her sit in silence, and then we slowly unpacked what had just happened. One of Cate's most obvious realizations was just how angry she felt. She was furious at how hard it felt to get money, much less keep it. Furthermore, she was outraged by human greed and enraged by the actions of people in her life regarding money. She was angry at how poorly her family members treated one another when it came to monetary transactions. Money had been used to manipulate and punish. There was never a sense of enough, and you could never ask for more. No wonder she cringed at the thought of raising her rates. Why would she ever subject herself to that?

As we dug deeper, we uncovered specific memories of watching her parents have heated arguments as they struggled to pay the bills. She remembered feeling there was never enough money to go around, much less to bring happiness and ease into her life. As a child, she felt confused about why her friends' families didn't seem to be going through the same struggles. She felt robbed of parts of her childhood and had been harboring anger and resentment toward money as a result.

Her anger revealed that Cate felt trapped and controlled by her circumstances. She felt like a part of herself had never matured, believing that a life with money could not be anything other than what she had experienced as a child. She wanted something different but did not know how to get there. Her anger was her way of rebelling, firmly declaring, "I've had enough!" But she had been so blinded by it that she hadn't been able to pave a new way to engage with money.

• MINI MOMENT •

What do I want to let go of in my relationship to money?

PRACTICE: Relax Your Grasping and Embody Wealth

What if the purpose of accruing wealth were less about profit and bottom lines and more about increasing the quality of meaningful life experiences and enhancing our ability to feel and embody joy?

As you take steps in this direction, wealth is less about becoming and staying rich and more about becoming and staying fulfilled. You do that by learning how to embody wealth instead of simply accumulating it. Ironically, when wealth requires you to integrate the rich tapestry of meaning in your life, talking about money stops being a cultural taboo and instead becomes a way to fill up your cup. Let's do a little practice to get a sense of how this feels.

Step 1: Clench Your Fists

Clench your fists for ten seconds. Notice how that feels, and then clench them again, this time for thirty seconds. Recognize the effort this takes. Now see if you can grip your fists tightly for an entire minute. This gives us a sense of the energy it takes to hold on to all your possessions. We do this far too often in our lives. When you feel stressed about money, you start grasping. You can almost be certain that you are clenching, possessing, or protecting your resources because you are afraid of losing them. And as you probably found out with this fist-clenching practice, we spend a lot of energy trying to keep our resources close to home.

Step 2: Extend Your Arms

The opposite is also true when you push money away. Extend your arms out as far as you can and hold them for thirty seconds. It takes focus and effort. Just as much energy is required to keep money at bay. Most of us tend to oscillate between the two, grasping or rejecting money. Often, our reactions to money are unconscious patterns we exhibit based on what we saw our parents do with money or the values we assign to it.

Come back to the premise that money is a tool used to express collective agreements among people. When we hold money for what it is and use that same energy to turn toward things we truly feel passionate about, we release the unconscious shackles money holds and free up resources to do our work in the world.

> **• MINI MOMENT •**
>
> *Clench your fists and ask yourself:* What am I holding on to perhaps too tightly in my life? Am I using money to do this?
>
> *Hold your arms out and ask:* What am I pushing away? How am I using money to push away?

Step 3: Open and Close

Now, clench your fists again, and let's practice opening them. Ball your hands tightly, but this time focus on our new definition of resources and wealth. Imagine that the most important resources you have are made of the meaningful moments in your life. Start to relax your fists and open your hands as you allow yourself to feel into these meaningful experiences. What lessons did you take away, who were you with, how did this change your relationships or the way you see yourself in the world? Continue to relax your hands and imagine what other opportunities for meaning are right around the corner. Notice how you can trust life to show up here. You have had meaningful moments in your life, and you will have them again.

From this place of trust, you can let go of the material resources you are holding on to. You know that material resources alone do not bring you meaning and joy, and you trust you know how to generate and access more meaning in your life when you want or need to.

This new, embodied approach to wealth helps us to relax. It offers a different experience of wealth — one based on trust in our innate power to create what we need in life. Our ability to generate meaning in our lives, rather than a stockpile of goods or services, should be the new bedrock of our sense of worth and definition of wealth.

Unlocking the Potential of Embodied Wealth

I hear clients tell me all the time that money feels too abstract, complicated, and unreal. A CW$ helps demystify money. It is a tool that cuts to the chase and sits us down in a one-to-one conversation with money, without any distractions or intermediaries. This is often the most revealing part.

We might not like to admit it, but we know that we bear a good deal of responsibility for our financial life. Admission is permission. When we acknowledge our own role in how our money life is playing out, we free up resources to design alternative routes and create a different financial future.

Practicing the power of enough, from both perspectives, helps you embrace a new paradigm — that of embodied wealth. Embodied wealth consists of experiencing wealth outside the constraints of your financial balance sheet and *rooting* yourself in the power of being and having enough, while also applying intentional boundaries in your personal and professional endeavors.

The heart of this transformative journey lies in the recognition that money is not in control — you are. It is not something to amass for accumulation's sake; it's something to use as a resource to design your unique definition of wealth, one that starts from the inside out. Inner economics precedes outer economics.

Your past does not shackle you, and your future is not predetermined by financial constraints. Money is not the ruler, but rather a resource; it is an instrument you wield to create the landscape of your wealth expression. You have the power to choose, create, and redefine wealth in every moment of your existence.

Embodied wealth is not confined to the digits in your bank account, and it transcends numerical values. It involves a profound metamorphosis — one of learning and practicing tools that nurture security and stability from within. This is a radical departure from the tedious hamster wheel of life, which is defined by productivity and earning more. It is a shift toward a more enriching human experience and a deeper trust that we can harness and access the resources we need.

What prevents you from embracing a more expanded version of wealth? Take a moment to introspect. If clarity eludes you, persist in asking the question. This territory may be unexplored, but the present moment is the perfect starting point.

Integration Is Key

Learning to have hard conversations is one of the most important skills we learn. But equally significant is learning how to recover and glean insights from what we hear.

One last thing: it doesn't matter how hard or easy it felt, whether it flowed or you drew a blank. Even sitting in the void and hearing crickets means something is happening. You are showing up to be in the conversation and creating space for whatever needs to be revealed.

Misusing the insights from your CW$ or handling them improperly can result in undesirable outcomes. If you're honest, what has money revealed to you so far? What have you let slip through the cracks? What aspects have you overlooked or left unaddressed? It is not about assigning blame; rather, it's an opportunity to own your feelings and recognize areas for improvement. Integration is about growth and self-awareness, essential steps in the journey toward establishing a healthier relationship with money and finding more joy.

Integration is not an invitation to wallow or get stuck in your emotions. Quite the contrary — to wallow is to indulge in help-lessness and remain committed to maintaining your current griev-ances. It solidifies a sense of victimhood, preventing you from experiencing liberation or positive change. The invitation with integration is to *feel* in order to *heal*.

Chapter 4 Takeaways

Unraveling the Complex Relationship with Money: This chap-ter delves into the stories of two clients, Jonathan and Cate, to explore the intricate and often emotional relationship individuals have with money. It highlights how past experiences, family nar-ratives, and unresolved emotions can significantly affect financial decision-making.

From Scared to Sacred: Jonathan's story emphasizes the impor-tance of addressing deep-seated emotions related to money, such as fear and unworthiness. The transformation from feeling scared to sacred involves recognizing the limitations of money in pro-viding true satisfaction and fulfillment. It encourages individuals to establish a sacred relationship with money that goes beyond material wealth.

Harnessing the Power of Anger: Cate's intense dialogue with money reveals the power of anger as a tool for self-reflection. Her CW$ emphasizes that anger, when channeled constructively, can illuminate areas where change is needed. Acknowledging and un-derstanding anger can lead to personal growth, empowering in-dividuals to reshape their financial landscape and cultivate a new sense of agency.

Embracing Limits as Leverage for Growth: Recognizing when you've had enough isn't a sign of failure, but rather a powerful indicator that it's time for change. By acknowledging and feeling into challenging emotions like anger and fear, you can understand your boundaries better. This process allows you to let go of what no longer serves you while also carrying forward the lessons learned. Embodying the power of enough means using these emotional signposts to assertively make the necessary adjustments, transforming discomfort into decisive action for personal growth.

Learning to Loosen Your Grip on Money: Shifting our perspective on wealth from mere accumulation to embodying meaningful experiences helps enhance the quality of our lives and cultivate joy. This involves recognizing and releasing unconscious patterns of grasping money or pushing it away, and instead, embracing a new definition of wealth centered around meaningful moments and relationships. By practicing openness and trust in our ability to generate meaning, we let go of the relentless pursuit of material resources and find fulfillment in the richness of our lived experiences.

PART 2

Embodying
WEALTH
and Cultivating
SATIATION

Chapter Five

EMBODIED WEALTH

Body, Mind, Heart, and Soul

Here's the hard truth, and one that we stated before — money is neither good nor bad but neutral. It is a mirror that reflects your relationship with the world around you. It does not define you. It guides you. Like a fair but determined coach, money is pushing you to become a better version of yourself. It is a social technology that can become a conduit for purpose, connection, and meaning when used with deliberate awareness and intent.

Mastering the art of speaking with money can be a profound self-discovery process. When used appropriately, it equips you to meet your needs, empower your actions, and realize your personal and professional ambitions. But as we've seen, there is a trap — the abundance-scarcity cycle. When you get lost in the loop of trying to acquire more and more money, you risk losing track of money's actual role in your life, which is to be a guide and mentor on your journey toward well-being.

Similar principles apply to wealth. It is not found in the static hoarding of assets but in the active cultivation of meaningful experiences. Wealth is more like a state of well-being that is constantly evolving and unfolding. It is the richness, the depth, and the personal significance you garner through varied experiences, reflections, and learnings.

But how do you do this? How do you escape the abundance-scarcity cycle and turn toward creating a more profound and joyous life? You embody abundance *and* meaning. Embodying abundance alone will not free you from a scarcity mindset. Abundance can help to counteract feelings of scarcity; but to move toward lasting wealth, you must digest the significant moments in your life. To do this, you must turn toward the experiences of meaning, like vitality, intimacy, and growth. Turning toward meaning moments like these allows you to shift your focus from simply solving for security to embodying satiation.

The journey toward satiation requires that one adopt a broader view than that offered by an abundance mindset. I invite you to lift your gaze from the abundance-scarcity cycle and envision a wider field of engagement, rooted in what I call the *meaning-fulfillment cycle*. The addition of this meaning-fulfillment cycle to the abundance-scarcity cycle is the *satiation paradigm*. In this new, embodied framework, your understanding of wealth is grounded in a basic sense of abundance in the world, as well as in a variety of meaningful experiences found in your *body*, *heart*, and *mind*. As you embody these experiences, you create meaning in your life, which feeds your *soul*. Soul, as referenced in these pages, is not some ghostlike entity but the lived experience of meaning in your life. The satiation paradigm points us toward the fulfillment found through a life lived in deep connection to your soul.

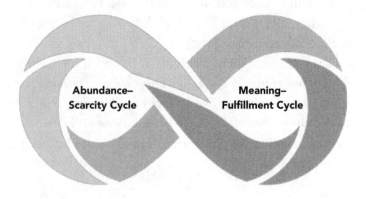

Abundance–
Scarcity Cycle

Meaning–
Fulfillment Cycle

Satiation Paradigm

Security concerns are not left behind in this new satiation paradigm. Life is full of transitions, traumas, and triumphs, and so the need to create and maintain abundance will never go away. For example, as you navigate stages in your life that demand financial change (e.g., having a baby, buying a home, paying for college, addressing long-term care needs), issues of security still take center stage. While the meaning-fulfillment cycle is distinct from the abundance-scarcity cycle that is so closely tied to issues like financial stability, physical health, and safety, these two cycles can never be fully separated. No matter how deeply you dive into the soul-oriented power of enough in your life, you will inevitably have to revisit concerns around abundance and scarcity, especially during times of transition and change.

But if you know what a satiation paradigm feels like and learn how to integrate it, you trust that you can make your way back. Over time, your ability to attend to matters of meaning will become more prominent. And as you integrate these meaningful experiences, they become embodied and compound, creating a new form of well-being — an experience of embodied wealth and satiation.

The meaning-fulfillment cycle originates from valuable experiences that arise out of the three centers: body (vitality-energy), heart (intimacy-vulnerability), and mind (growth-development). Your journey with meaning can lead to profound experiences that connect you to your core essence or soul. You can think of these deep experiences — what I call *moments of meaning* — as spiritual in nature. One of the most unwavering spiritual experiences in my life is the power of enough. This enduring sense of enoughness finds ways to express itself through my body, heart, and mind as meaningful experiences compound and fill me up. They are moments that stop me in my tracks, infusing me with a genuine sentiment that I love my life. As you start to situate the abundance-scarcity cycle in its appropriate place and connect to joy and meaning, you'll discover your own unique expression of embodied wealth.

> ● MINI MOMENT ●
>
> Where in my life am I connected to my soul?
> Where do I already experience the power of enough?

Embodying Wealth through the Power of Enough

In a world where the pursuit of more is often conflated with the pursuit of happiness, we lose track of a subtle and profound aspect of our being: the power of enough. This power is grounded in the understanding that wealth is not created by accumulating possessions, but rather through incorporating the rich moments of meaning that resonate with personal significance throughout our lives.

In chapter 1, we made a distinction between finite games in search of scarce resources and infinite games where resources are multifaceted and universally available. In the finite game, we are aiming to stabilize our financial health, which is a necessary aspect of our overall sense of prosperity. In contrast, in the infinite game of wealth and well-being, we orient toward moments of meaning.

In this light, the power of enough becomes a transformative force, converting your metric of success from security to satiation. As you begin to embody wealth in your life, you gain access to your own unique power of enough. As this journey deepens, it encourages you to shift from accumulating what is superfluous to cherishing what is essential. The power of enough requires embodying those nonmaterial resources that nourish your body, fill your heart, and expand your mind, ensuring that when you reach the end of your days, you can reflect on how meaningfully you've lived.

This newfound wealth, grounded in a paradigm of satiation, transcends your bank accounts and nurtures a sense of sufficiency and contentment that can become your natural way of being in the world — a life lived in deep connection to the meaningful moments that make up the experience of soul. The following sections clarify the different kinds of meaning we find in our lives, helping to create the power of enough and a sense of embodied wealth for ourselves and our loved ones.

Embodying Wealth, Experiencing Well-Being

There are three centers always available to us in our embodied life: our body, heart, and mind. Seeing your lived experience through these centers is deceptively simple. But it is the simplicity of these practices that allows us to explore the depths of significance of our lives and souls. The concept of embodied wealth captures the entirety of the human experience, integrating important experiences from physical, emotional, intellectual, and spiritual domains into a nuanced form of riches.

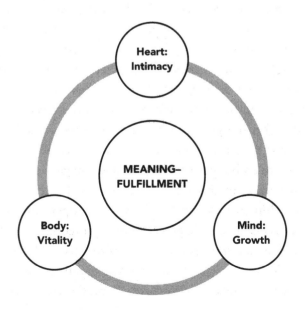

In the body, embodied wealth is gained through the grounding sensations of touch, the tenderness of shared interactions, and the vitality that comes from physical movement and engagement with the world. Each dance, each workout, each embrace, each meal, and each breath has the potential for profound significance. These experiences of vitality in the body center create moments of meaning that can morph into creativity, excellence, blissful ecstasy, and rapture. Our bodies, often neglected in the pursuit of material wealth, are reservoirs of knowledge and insight, understanding and health, deeply capable of experiencing strength, joy, pleasure, balance, and the genuine satisfaction of being alive.

Heart-centered experiences contribute to embodied wealth through the deepening of our relationships, creating intimacy in our lives. These are communal and shared moments of meaning that emerge from experiences of connection, belonging, and participation. They can feel like love, friendship, compassion, empathy, and belonging. Giving and receiving heart-centered interactions helps to fortify our deep well of social and emotional well-being. This kind of heart-oriented wealth comes from laughter shared with friends, the comfort of a loved one's presence, and the bonds that endure through times of hardship, offering a warmth and richness that material wealth cannot replicate.

In the realm of the mind, embodied wealth is formed through experiences rooted in a growth mindset. It is through such experiences that we find the mental strength and resilience to overcome challenges. Experiences of the mind can feel like moments of self-esteem, purpose, and freedom. The mind center tends to be future oriented. Meaning can be found as we challenge ourselves to move toward a goal, purpose, or ambition. Growth comes as we hone our abilities in critical thinking, creativity, intellectual rigor, and wisdom. These experiences of growth can also arise as we develop our self-awareness, improve our ability to focus, and align with our values and ideals, like beauty, integrity, compassion, and truth. This dimension of wealth is not about the accumulation of facts but the integration of knowledge into a framework that guides our decisions, molds our character, and brings wisdom and insight into our lives.

Each of these centers has its own expression of meaning. In the body, we are in a constant relationship with the energy we feel in any given moment. It is an expression that can lead to fatigue and exhaustion just as easily as it can lead to resilience, composure, and strength. No matter the experience, whether it is agitating or enlivening, it can be integrated and embodied as vitality.

In the heart, we experience vulnerability through diverse interactions with everyone we meet. These experiences can span from anxiety provoking to heartwarming and beyond. As we move through these exchanges, we learn about trust and belonging. No matter the feeling or whether we decide to externalize it or keep it private, our heart-centered journey always leads toward greater intimacy with ourselves and the world around us.

In the mind, we become motivated by development in all domains of life. They can include anything from innovation and freedom to truth and harmony. Whatever the impulse, our unique set of values calls us to develop our character through moments of growth.

When considered together, the expressions of our lives start to come into focus: In the realm of the body, we are motivated by the experience of vitality and energy; the heart-oriented journey is one of intimacy and vulnerability; and the mind center is instrumental to growth and development. As we integrate the lessons of these experiences of meaning into our lives, we experience embodied wealth.

As we nurture these diverse ways of experiencing and creating depth, we unlock our own unique gifts. This journey is part of a richer involvement with meaning — the spiritual life of the soul, which takes on an essence of fulfillment. Diving into our depths enables us to live fully, with a sense of completeness that material wealth alone could never offer. The embodied wealth we discover in this soul-centered approach to life moves us away from the scarcity-oriented approach to life by connecting the abundance-scarcity cycle to a new meaning-fulfillment cycle. This journey through meaning toward self-realization introduces us to the truest form of wealth that exists.

• MINI MOMENT •

How do I experience wealth in my body?
How do I experience wealth in my heart?
How do I experience wealth in my mind?
How do these experiences of wealth feed my soul?

Taking a Closer Look at Your Energetic Centers

Across cultures and throughout history, humans have sought to understand the relationship between the physical body and intangible aspects of our being, such as emotions, thoughts, and the soul. Many traditions have developed systems that map these connections, recognizing the existence of specific bodily centers or energy points that serve as focal points for various aspects of our experience.

The theory of energy centers with specific physical, emotional, and spiritual qualities, known as the chakra system, originated from India's traditions. Traditional Chinese medicine recognizes the flow of qi (energy) through meridians connecting various organs and bodily functions. Additionally, three energy centers called *dantians* regulate physical vitality, emotional balance, and spiritual awareness. The use of such systems has been adopted throughout the course of human history.

By exploring the body, heart, and mind as distinct yet interconnected centers, we can gain a deeper understanding of how our experiences in these realms contribute to our sense of embodied wealth and well-being. This framework encourages us to cultivate meaning and fulfillment not only through material abundance but also through the integration of profound experiences that resonate throughout our physical, emotional, and intellectual lives, all of which feed our spiritual being.

Embodying Abundance and Overcoming Scarcity

As you learned in chapter 1, traditional definitions of wealth and economics revolve around the idea of overcoming scarcity. Whether scarcity involves food, companionship, or prestige, traditional approaches to wealth management offer a solution that focuses on creating abundance by accumulating more resources. To feel wealthy in this traditional model, you must always be creating access to more resources. When resources are in ample supply in this model, scarcity is diminished, and as a result, we should feel wealthy. But solving for scarcity alone does not create enduring wealth. It addresses only the areas where we feel lack.

The abundance-scarcity cycle is an attempt to alleviate scarcity through accumulation of resources. This is where a lot of people get stuck; because the cycle fails to address our underlying needs for depth and meaning, it leads to a continuous and unsatisfying pursuit of more.

If you lack shoes, buying the first pair solves an immediate problem. Buying ten more does not. In fact, at some point, we experience a diminishing return on our next purchase. Adding more shoes to your closet, an extra car, a bigger home, or a second home requires you to make more money. And these added possessions can create other kinds of work, such as care and upkeep.

The best way to embody abundance is to do the important work of clarifying how much and what types of resources you require for financial stability. This brings clarity and transparency to your different centers, freeing up awareness, attention, and essential resources for meaning and fulfillment. Financial planning is an important tool and invaluable process that sheds light on how much you need to earn, save, spend, gift, and invest to align your material life with your value and security needs. But you must be careful not to get stuck in a never-ending loop of abundance and scarcity. Financial practices are important, but alone they are never going to be enough to bring lasting contentment. To be fulfilled you must also turn toward the meaning that arises from our three centers — body, heart, and mind. These soul-centric experiences of meaning connect us to our deep well that is our own unique experience of the power of enough.

One way to cultivate an abundance mindset alongside financial planning is to regularly practice affirmations, gratitude journaling, and developing resilience. Resource-mapping helps us acknowledge and appreciate the diverse forms of wealth we already possess, like community support and personal strengths. By creating a visual map or list of the various forms of support, skills, and assets at your disposal, you can shift your mindset from one of lack to one of gratitude and sufficiency. And as you engage in resource-mapping, you might discover untapped sources of abundance and resilience, such as a supportive community, a unique talent, or an inner reservoir of courage and determination.

Vision boards are also a popular tool in personal development to visualize desired life outcomes, often using images or symbols of personal success as inspiration. Proponents of this practice argue that regularly focusing on and visualizing your ideal life helps to cultivate an abundance mindset, shifting your thoughts and emotions from a state of lack to one of prosperity and possibility. However, this practice often emphasizes material wealth over deeper fulfillment, potentially trapping individuals in an abundance-scarcity cycle. To achieve lasting wealth, it's important to also integrate personal growth, meaningful relationships, and contributions to others into our visions of success.

The Way of the Body: Embodying Vitality

The expression of vitality, central to the body center, plays a crucial role in transitioning from a mindset focused on material abundance to one that values energy and aliveness. Vitality is experienced subjectively as heightened energy and liveliness, yet it also has objective markers that can be measured to gauge health and well-being. Engaging in activities that nourish and energize the body — such as mindful movement, balanced nutrition, and sufficient rest — helps establish a cycle of vitality that fuels further growth and engagement. This approach shifts our focus from external acquisitions to nurturing our inherent energy, laying the foundation for a sustainable sense of fulfillment that resonates through all aspects of life.

Engaging in activities such as running, dancing, tai chi, or any other active sports can improve both physical strength and flexibility while also enhancing our connection to and appreciation of our bodies. Similarly, adopting a diet rich in energizing foods and maintaining a healthy relationship with eating can significantly boost our vitality. Equally important is prioritizing rest, which can be achieved through practices such as restorative yoga and therapeutic massage, allowing our bodies ample time to recover and rejuvenate. Moreover, spending time outdoors can profoundly revitalize our mental and physical well-being, reminding us of the beauty and abundance that the natural world offers. These practices, when performed regularly, build a robust foundation of health and vitality, enabling us to lead lives filled with energy and purpose.

True embodiment of vitality requires more than occasional practice; it necessitates daily rituals that honor and respond to the body's needs. Listening to our body's signals and responding with appropriate activities and rest allows us to maintain a dynamic balance that supports ongoing vitality. By cultivating a positive and appreciative relationship with our physical selves, we move away from being judgmental and toward a more nurturing approach. Ultimately, as we align our daily practices with our values and integrate them into our routines, we break free from the cycle of scarcity and tap into a deeper source of fulfillment, contributing to a holistic sense of a rich life and enabling us to develop a deeper connection with ourselves and the world around us.

While our basic biology is universal, the way your body loves to move through the world is unique to you. I encourage you to find practices that help you to uncover the sensuous life your body is ready to live. Get out there, start dancing, and see what this vital aspect of your person is yearning to teach you.

> • MINI MOMENT •
>
> What practices do I naturally gravitate toward in the scope of my body?

The Way of the Heart: Embodying Intimacy

The heart center is pivotal to embodied wealth, serving as a conduit for emotional depth, connection, and meaning within the cycle of intimacy-vulnerability. The heart is essential for experiencing intimacy — the deep sense of closeness, trust, and belonging that nourishes our souls and enriches our lives. To cultivate true intimacy, embrace vulnerability by opening to a broad spectrum of human emotions and experiences. By engaging with the heart center, we access a rich source of meaning derived from the intimate relationships we nurture with ourselves, others, and the broader world.

The interplay between intimacy and vulnerability arises in our willingness and courage to dive into our capacity for deep, authentic connection. When we allow ourselves to be fully seen and known in our humanity, we create the necessary conditions for true intimacy to flourish.

Vulnerability is crucial in the heart center. It acts as a gateway to authentic connection, allowing us to be fully seen and known. However, embracing vulnerability requires courage, as it involves shedding protective barriers and exposing our true selves. This process can be profound, but if we hide behind masks of perfection or indifference, we risk becoming trapped in isolation and disconnection.

Practices such as developing emotional intelligence, engaging in authentic communication, and cultivating compassion and forgiveness are vital. They help us navigate our emotions in a healthy and constructive manner, enhancing our relationships and overall emotional health.

Ultimately, the journey through the heart center is about transforming our emotional landscape, from one of scarcity to one of richness and connection. This transformation is not just about personal growth; it has a communal aspect, enhancing our relationships and improving the lives of those around us. By prioritizing emotional well-being and vulnerability, we tap into the heart's full potential, fostering a life of deep emotional fulfillment and sustained intimate connections.

The way of the heart is a path of courage, compassion, and connection. By understanding the heart center, engaging in practices that cultivate intimacy and vulnerability, and integrating them into our daily lives, we open ourselves to a transformative experience of love, belonging, and emotional richness. As we embark on this journey of embodying intimacy, we discover the true depths of our own hearts and the hearts of those around us.

• MINI MOMENT •

What practices am I naturally attracted to in the realm of my heart?

The Way of the Mind: Embodying Growth

The mind center plays a crucial role in intellectual and personal growth. It acts as a catalyst that enables us to acquire new skills, knowledge, perspectives, and insights, thereby catapulting our lives beyond the mere accumulation of material wealth. By continuously developing our cognitive and intellectual faculties, we access a source of wealth that enhances our understanding of ourselves and the world, fostering a deep sense of fulfillment and purpose.

When we embrace challenges as opportunities for growth and view setbacks as valuable lessons, we create a virtuous cycle of continuous improvement and self-discovery. However, if we become complacent or resistant to change, we risk stagnation and a sense of intellectual poverty that can limit our overall well-being.

To actualize the potential of the mind center, we engage in practices that stimulate and challenge our intellectual capacities. Visualization and imagination are powerful tools within this sphere, harnessing our creative potential and aligning our energies with our deepest aspirations. Together they create vivid mental images that foster growth and transformation. Developing a growth mindset teaches us to view intelligence and abilities as malleable qualities that can be harnessed through effort and perseverance. This perspective encourages us to embrace challenges, persist through difficulties, and see failures as opportunities for growth. For example, budgeting and cash flow planning provide our minds with clear considerations and parameters on how to best allocate resources given what we earn, spend, invest, gift, and save.

The way of the mind is an invitation to embrace growth, learning, and self-discovery as essential elements of a rich and fulfilling life. Establishing routines that encourage learning, surrounding ourselves with inspiring individuals, and stepping outside our comfort zones are all crucial steps in this journey. By nurturing our mind's potential, we align our intellectual growth with our deepest values and aspirations. This can contribute to a holistic sense of true wealth that celebrates the richness of the human experience and the profound power of enough.

> • MINI MOMENT •
>
> What practices do I naturally implement with my mind?

Embodying Meaning: The Role of Satiation and Soul in Our Lives

The final transition in this new definition of wealth moves toward the soul-centered meaning-fulfillment cycle. In this cycle, the pursuit of wealth changes to seeking deep personal fulfillment and satisfaction through activities that align with one's values and purpose. Depth of experience takes precedence over all else. This generates the state of being rich and brings us to the soul center.

The soul is the source of meaning and the core of our being. Here, we discover the true essence of wealth, not as an accumulation of material possessions or financial assets but as an alignment with our values and aspirations. By tapping into the soul, we experience satiation — feeling "enough" — which empowers us to live authentically with joy and purpose. This alignment with our soul guides us through life's challenges and opportunities with grace.

When you connect with your soul, you tap into a wellspring of wisdom and guidance that helps you navigate the challenges and opportunities of life with poise, commitment, and resilience. Your soul speaks to you through your intuition, dreams, and moments of profound insight and inspiration. By learning to listen to the whispers of the soul, you open to a deeper understanding of your place in the world and your true purpose for being here.

The meaning-fulfillment cycle is a dynamic interplay between your search for meaning and your experience of fulfillment. The key is learning to harness wisdom from all your centers (body, heart, and mind) to cultivate a deep and abiding connection with your soul. Several practices can help. Self-reflection and introspection can reveal what is important. Engaging in activities that align with your core values and purpose generates a sense of harmony and coherence. Meditation, prayer, or time in nature can plug you into a deeper sense of belonging and purpose that transcends your individual self. Or practicing gratitude and appreciation for the blessings in your life can shift your focus from what is lacking to what is already present and meaningful.

Practice and integration are key. This involves carving out time to engage with your chosen practice and setting aside time for reflection, journaling, or creative expression. It also means making conscious choices about how you spend your time, energy, and resources, prioritizing activities and relationships that bring you fulfillment while letting go of those that drain or deplete you.

Embodying meaning and fulfillment through your soul is the ultimate expression of embodied wealth. We begin to see wealth as a state of being that arises from a deep sense of connection, purpose, and fulfillment, rather than something to hoard or accumulate. As we align our lives with the whispers of our soul and embody the power of enough, we discover joy, connection, and purpose that infuses every moment with richness and beauty. By embracing the way of the soul, we become cocreators of a world that is more just, compassionate, and abundant for all, one where the true essence of wealth is measured not by what we have but by who we are and how we choose to live.

As you come to understand the shift from scarcity to satiation, you see that while an abundance of money can ensure you can pay your bills on time, help you buy a home, and bring comfort, luxury, and experiences, it does not guarantee happiness. Real wealth requires an ongoing commitment to growth and meaning. Our definition of wealth must include resources that offer opportunities to create moments of meaning. By turning toward a definition of wealth that includes an emphasis on embodiment and satiation, you find that you don't need more than everyone else to feel wealthy. Instead, you gain access to an entirely new array of resources that lie at your fingertips.

Chapter 5 Takeaways

True Wealth Is Embodied: Embodied wealth goes beyond the accumulation of material possessions and financial assets. By tapping into the wisdom of our three bodily centers — the body, heart, and mind — we can cultivate a deeper sense of meaning, purpose, and fulfillment in all areas of our lives, including our relationship with money. The experience of meaning that arises from each of these centers connects us to the life of our soul.

There Are Many Centers of Well-Being: Each of the three centers offers a unique pathway to embodied wealth. The body center is oriented toward vitality and aims to increase our overall energy by teaching us to prioritize our physical well-being and to make financial choices that support our health and resilience.

The heart center invites us to align our financial lives with our deepest values of love, connection, and compassion, using our resources to nurture our relationships and our sense of belonging.

The mind center encourages us to cultivate a growth mindset around money, embrace challenges as opportunities for learning and development, and set financial goals that align with our deepest values. This contributes to a sense of wealth that transcends material possessions and reflects the true richness of the human experience.

Defining Embodied Wealth: Embodied wealth is about recognizing and experiencing the power of enough — the understanding that true wealth arises not from having more but from being more fully alive and connected to others, the world around us, and our souls. By aligning our financial lives with our deepest values and aspirations, and by using our resources in ways that create meaning and purpose, we can tap into an inexhaustible source of spiritual meaning that enhances us on every level — physically, emotionally, and mentally. In this way, we become not just consumers of wealth but creators and stewards of a richer, more beautiful world for ourselves and for all beings.

Chapter Six

RECOGNIZING THAT NEEDS ARE NATURAL

Designing Your Life

You have needs, and so do I. Recognizing our needs is as important as breathing. Understanding what they are and how to satisfy them gives us the essential ingredients to work with when designing our life. They are as basic as food, shelter, and companionship and as refined as curiosity, leisure, and belonging. All play a critical role in our well-being.

Yet while needs are universal, the ways we meet them can be very personal. Discovering how to best satisfy our needs is key to practicing satiation and requires creating a visual map. This map guides us in constructing a life aligned with our deepest values, bridging the gap between mere survival and thriving. By creating such a map, we link the concept of wealth to well-being, designing a life that is rich in satisfaction and meaning. The journey toward satiation is all about discovering how to nurture our core sense of self with what genuinely fulfills us. Put simply, we can choose to live by design, not by default.

The discussion around the abundance-scarcity cycle from previous chapters extends wealth beyond the narrow confines of profit. We move past this cycle and into fulfillment by creating a foundational sense of security in our lives, shifting from a per-petual pursuit of more things to one of deep satisfaction. This transition is pivotal: when you identify what is truly meaningful, you can craft a life map that resonates with your values and aspirations. This is not a subtle shift but a transformative one. Operating within the security paradigm often leads to a sense of constriction and helplessness. Embracing a satiation paradigm fosters empowerment, agency, and self-efficacy.

Designing your life requires first acknowledging you have needs, knowing what they are, and prioritizing synergistic strategies. This is easier said than done, and this chapter demystifies the process by shedding light on the evolution of needs and highlighting the differences between *needs* and *satisfiers*. Needs are what drive us, and satisfiers are the ways we satisfy them that align with our path and progress.

The Taboo around Money and Needs

Talking about money is often considered taboo in our culture. This stems from deep cultural norms that entangle conversations about money with sensitive and highly private issues, touching on tender emotions, social comparison, jealously, fear of judgment, and shame.

As we saw with conversations with money in chapter 3, navigating our relationship with money can be daunting. But it becomes even more so when money intersects with what we require to be happy and healthy — our human needs. Because our needs are muddled by our conversations with money (those we have and those we don't have), we are reluctant to claim them as needs, even though they are essential to our health and well-being. These important discussions remain stigmatized and we stay silent, which leaves us feeling isolated, confused, and misunderstood.

Even when we allow ourselves to claim certain human needs as essentials, we usually stay well within the bounds of security. We prioritize strategies that optimize our resources in service of our basic needs (food, shelter, clothing), and we hesitate when it comes to satiation-oriented needs like purpose, strong relationships, and creative expression. To move forward, we need to affirm that a variety of human needs are not only natural but essential.

Human Needs Are Natural

As soon as we are born, our ability to bond and recognize the importance of relationships begins. As babies, we knew to signal when we were hungry, tired, or longing to be held. These signals have existed within each of us since inception, but cultural norms have shamed us into pretending that even our most basic needs are whims or luxuries, causing undue shame and a sense of greed for simply having them. The misconception that fulfilling our basic needs is a luxury only adds to this misdirected guilt. Acknowledging and addressing our natural needs isn't a privilege but a critical aspect of honoring our humanity.

To create sustainable wealth, you must feel at home with yourself. This requires that you gain a deep understanding of what is required to feel satisfied. Life is full of changes and challenges, and many of these will entail that we return our attention to stabilizing our financial health. But if we also hold wealth as something to embody rather than to accumulate, we free ourselves from the abundance-scarcity cycle our cultural conversations around money and needs have become stuck in. This in turn allows us to connect to something larger. And as you make this shift, your management of resources includes strategies to elevate needs like intimacy and meaning alongside ways to improve and optimize the financial investments in your portfolio.

Take a moment to breathe this all in. So many things that you secretly desire, but are afraid to even admit to yourself, are actually universal human needs. Your ongoing health and well-being demand that you understand these needs so that you can feel at home with yourself. The clearer your pathways toward purpose and self-expression become, the more you feel at home. As you align with what brings intimacy and meaning into your life, a newfound depth of relationship naturally arises with everyone and everything around you. Let's take a pulse to understand where you are on this journey.

• MINI MOMENT •

What are some of the needs I have that, when satisfied, help me thrive?
What do I honestly think and feel about the fact that I have these needs in the first place?

Embracing your human needs as natural helps you to create a clear and direct pathway toward feeling at home in yourself. Now, let's turn back the clock and see where the conversation about needs began.

Needs as a Path for Self-Actualization

In 1943, psychologist Abraham Maslow published his seminal work, the paper "A Theory of Human Motivation." It focused on a few key themes. He articulated that our motivations are an intrinsic part of our being — our "integrated wholeness of the organism," as he phrased it. Seen through the lens of embodied wealth, this suggests that our drive stems from a deeply rooted, organic quest to find meaning and infuse it into our lives.

Maslow categorized needs into two primary types: basic needs, which he aligned with our survival and security; and growth needs, which propel us toward a flourishing state of human existence outside the abundance-scarcity cycle. This was the real contribution of Maslow's work — to add needs that are aimed toward *self-actualization.* He argued that we must "enable people to become healthy and effective in their own style." Our potential is reached not merely through survival but by cultivating our unique capacities. Thus, he guided our focus from mere security toward a richer, satisfaction-oriented approach to life.

Somehow, we still haven't caught up. Popular culture maintains taboos around conversation about money, which means we don't talk about even our most basic human needs.

Sometime in the 1960s, a management consultant firm reimagined Maslow's theory of human motivation as a pyramid, an idea that has continued to color his work to this day. The theory was turned into a rigid hierarchy and then drew criticism for being inflexible. Most people are familiar with this pyramid, even though it distorts Maslow's original intent. The pyramid shape mistakenly gives the impression that we are playing a game with specific levels to achieve. We have gotten stuck on the notion that there is a particular order toward self-actualization, which traps us in a fixed mindset where we play a finite game with winners and losers.

Maslow didn't see growth-oriented needs as luxuries for a privileged few; he understood them as vital for everyone's well-being. Growth-oriented satiation needs are important for the health and well-being of every person on the planet. They are not luxury goods but necessary sustenance.

There is no straight line that will help you win the game. It is an infinite game where the goal is to learn and embrace your potential for self-actualization. And as important as growth-oriented needs are, we don't recognize them as essential and universal human needs, like food and shelter. Finding your purpose is as vital for humanity's potential as having access to adequate food.

Maslow did not envision our development as a ladder to climb. Instead, he viewed our journey toward meaning as a dynamic process and interplay of experiences, where triumphs and tragedies alike present opportunities for growth and insight.

Imagine organizing needs within a framework of connected cycles or spokes on a wheel, rather than a pyramid. This helps us to focus our intentions on cultivating growth, vitality, intimacy, and abundance.

In chapter 2, we introduced Michael Easter's research on how we are hardwired to seek more, even when those behaviors are at odds with our well-being. He emphasizes that we have gotten stuck in the abundance-scarcity cycle because of our increasing desire for material possessions. He uses the term *scarcity loop* and argues that it is baked into our experience of the world at an evolutionary level. After we undergo something pleasurable, dopamine is released in our body. This creates a loop, where we either seek or anticipate seeking that pleasing experience again. In other words, we have not been wired to enjoy; we have been wired to seek, and we keep looking for something more.

We can't escape the scarcity loop, as it plays a role in our survival. We have evolved to always seek. But if you go after meaningful experiences within a larger paradigm, you can leverage your evolutionary imperative to seek participation in something greater and, as a result, find purpose. The key is to learn to embody these meaningful experiences, not just acquire a portfolio of spiritual tools and techniques. By embodying your being, you can feel satisfaction and the sense of having enough.

For Maslow, we are always in a state of growth and becoming, driven to self-actualize. One out of every seven adults in the world is struggling to afford food and shelter. While this is an ongoing problem that desperately needs to be solved, it is important to note that six out of every seven adults are able to meet their basic needs.

I would guess that even though you are part of the six in seven who have their basic needs met, you still find yourself in the abundance-scarcity cycle a lot. Why is it that we still feel poor when we have so much? Or said differently, if you have plenty of food, decent shelter, basic connections, and some amount of self-esteem, why do you find yourself fighting a nagging sense of scarcity? The reality is that you cannot buy your way out of your hardwired need to seek for more. No matter how many resources you accumulate, it is the pursuit rather than the consumption that motivates us in the abundance-scarcity cycle.

Maslow points us to an "inner core." I would call this the well filled with power of enough. In this well, we find all the aspects that are unique not only to you but also to every other individual. Growth and self-actualization are made possible to the extent that you can accept and express your inner core. According to Maslow, when this inner core is expressed, "becoming ceases for a moment and its promissory notes are cashed in the form of ultimate rewards — the peak experiences, in which time disappears and hopes are fulfilled." This speaks to the integration of abundance, intimacy, growth, and meaning. And when you experience this integration, your inner core becomes a deep well of satiation from which you can draw to experience your power of enough.

Instead of focusing on people's disruptive or problematic behavior, Maslow expanded the focus of psychology by turning toward the study of healthy behaviors and identifying strategies to support personal growth and well-being. He shifted the focus from what makes us deficient to what brings us joy, pleasure, and fulfillment. His work shed light on some of the main questions of human existence — namely, What are we after, and how do we prioritize our resources to get there?

* MINI MOMENT *

Money aside, what brings me a sense of fulfillment and joy in my life?

Maslow died in 1970. Toward the end of his life, he became more critical of capitalism. He lamented that much of our economic production was focused on fulfilling our most basic necessities while ignoring people's psychological and spiritual needs. This book is one answer to his concerns that we adopt a more holistic and embodied approach to our relationship to money and wealth. Maslow had a true vision of what it means to be fully self-actualized, and he postulated that at the height of economic production, society would support just that. Despite living in a world of unimagined abundance, we still seem to be trying to figure this out.

Toward Satiation:
Transforming Needs to Satisfiers

Manfred Max-Neef was a Chilean economist teaching at the University of California, Berkeley, in the 1960s, just as Maslow was ending his career. In 2003, I had the privilege of taking a course with Max-Neef at Schumacher College in the UK. He encouraged us to take a close look at our relationship to needs. This was extremely uncomfortable for me. I had to face my own prejudice and acknowledge that it felt threatening to explore my needs. It was the first time I consciously recognized that I had needs and that it was OK to acknowledge and embrace them.

Max-Neef highlighted that even though human needs are consistent across cultures, the way we satisfy these needs differs. He called the strategies we use to fulfill our needs *satisfiers* and emphasized the importance of clearly defining these approaches as a path to sustainable growth. Each of us is born into a unique financial and social reality, thus our starting points for creating wealth may be very different. There are so many things in life that we can't control. Common wisdom tells us to focus on what we can. Designing your life to promote your individual approach to wealth gives you agency and power to choose which strategies to implement, when, and for what needs.

If we let go of our collective judgment of needs and recognize that they have an important role to play, we can turn our attention to what matters most: recognizing that we have the power, ability, and responsibility to learn how to design unique satisfiers to meet our needs. We must understand this simple yet potent point: needs are natural, and we have the power to design better ways to satisfy them.

I'll offer one last point from Max-Neef before we jump into learning about satisfiers. He argued that contemporary society was so focused on creating new goods and services that we lost sight of the most important end goal: learning how to be human. This is a crucial lesson to learn to be able to embody wealth. You have the power to design your life, enabling you to achieve deeper fulfillment while more easily accessing the diversity of your ideas in your mind, the depth of emotions in your heart, and the vitality of your body. You have to reclaim your humanness. Embracing embodiment allows us to address the abundance-scarcity cycle that ensnares so much of the modern world. We can embody the infinite experiential resources that help us create intimacy and meaning in our lives.

Reflect on the resources that resonate with you the most. You may either use the examples in the list on the next page or write your own.

• MINI MOMENT •

What strengths and capacities do I naturally possess?
What resources do I want more of?
How can I use some of the resources I naturally have to help build what I feel weakest in?

LIST OF RESOURCES FOR INSPIRATION

Ability
Ambition
Attentiveness
Authenticity
Availability
Boldness
Breadth
Candor
Caution
Clarity
Confidence
Consistency
Contentment
Courage
Creativity
Decisiveness
Dependability
Depth
Determination
Devotion
Diligence
Empathy
Endurance
Enthusiasm
Entrepreneurship
Experience
Fairness
Faith
Firmness
Flexibility

Freedom
Generosity
Gentleness
Gratitude
Honesty
Humility
Individuality
Initiative
Insight
Integrity
Joy
Kindness
Knowledge
Loyalty
Optimism
Passion
Patience
Perception
Perseverance
Persuasion
Power
Purpose
Resourcefulness
Sensitivity
Sincerity
Technical skills
Transparency
Vision
Vulnerability
Wisdom

Satisfiers Help Create Meaning in Our Lives

Satisfiers are the strategies we employ to meet our needs, tapping into both our external and internal resources. The greater the supply of internal capabilities and financial means, the more options you have in designing your life.

As Max-Neef suggested, satisfiers help you to distinguish between your needs and the different ways you address them. Satisfiers stem from your culture, environment, passion, and individual sense of meaning. Identifying how you uniquely satisfy your needs brings intention to your life. It invokes responsibility and participation, asking you to step up to the plate.

Yet not all satisfiers allow us to embody wealth in the same way. Some satisfiers are extremely punctual and satisfy a particular security-oriented need (like paying a utility bill), while others satisfy several needs at once. A vacation with your family can nourish not only your need for time off and leisure but also your need to foster intimacy with your loved ones. In this way, satisfiers can address issues of security and abundance, as well as your desire for significant moments in your life.

It is your job to identify the best ways to satisfy your needs. If you give that task to someone else, you relinquish your power by believing that others have a better grasp on what you require to meet your needs. The more you pay attention to your choice of satisfiers, the more you grow and sustain your sense of agency.

Your setting has a lot of influence on how you satisfy your needs. For example, do you live in a fast-paced environment that emphasizes productivity, or somewhere leisure is prioritized and valued? Are you part of a multigenerational household, extended community, or nuclear family? What political systems are you exposed to? How physically safe do you feel in your environment? What level of privilege do you have based on your gender, sexual orientation, or skin color?

All these factors influence how we think and feel about possible satisfiers. Now, with the digital revolution and accessible travel, we interact cross-culturally more than ever before. We are challenging our collective norms and dreaming up new possibilities. We can use a wide variety of satisfiers to fulfill them.

Different Ways to Satisfy

Below are some examples of types of satisfiers. Understanding their differences is important. It can help you make better decisions about what strategies best fulfill your needs, knowing that in some cases, one approach might appease one need while depleting another.

- **Singular satisfiers** fulfill only one need and are neutral regarding the satisfaction of others. For example, brushing your teeth meets the need for health upkeep and hygiene, but few of us experience creativity, freedom, or connection while doing so. Or a house alarm can address a need for safety, but that is basically it.

- **Inhibiting satisfiers** are the ways we oversatisfy one need while hindering our ability to meet others. For example, an overprotective parent can think they are carrying out the need for protection by instituting strict rules in their household. But this can also stifle the space their teenager requires to explore their needs of identity, freedom, belonging, and connection. Conversely, living in a gated community might fulfill a sense of security, but it may also block the organic and spontaneous interactions with others that foster a sense of belonging and community.

- **Violators** are strategies that we think help satiate a need but may detract from real and lasting fulfillment. For example, using retail therapy to satisfy a need for leisure can become another need: to work more to pay off the higher credit card bill created by the shopping spree. Or if you choose to go to loud live concerts without earplugs to satisfy your love of music and creativity, at some point your hearing will suffer. What seemed to feed you in one moment detracts from your physical well-being in the long run. Violators are negative satisfiers because they feed one part of you at the expense of another. They make it more difficult to truly feel satisfied in the long term.

- **Pseudo satisfiers** are strategies that claim to satisfy a need but have little or no effect on doing so. For example, obtaining status symbols may initially boost one's self-esteem and identity, but there is always the danger of getting absorbed in them and forgetting who you really are.

- **Synergistic satisfiers** are strategies that satisfy a given need while simultaneously contributing to the satisfaction of others. For example, doing work you love can satisfy your need for financial stability while also addressing your need for connection, understanding, learning, and participation. In one of Max-Neef's most famous examples, breastfeeding is a synergistic satisfier because it not only provides nutritional sustenance but also fosters protection, affection, and belonging.

Imagine a world where you became skilled at identifying and using synergistic satisfiers. You would improve how you generate and employ resources, prioritizing the methods that satisfy more than one need at a time. As with moments of meaning, synergistic satisfiers help satisfaction build on itself, feeding into a deep sense of agency that you can design your life.

• MINI MOMENT •

What is one example in my life of each of the five ways I typically satisfy needs (singular, inhibiting, violator, pseudo, and synergistic)?

Satisfiers are like tools in the toolbox: some are sharper and better suited to certain tasks than others. One of the best pieces of advice I can give you when working with satisfiers is to approach your engagement with them through a lens of unconditional acceptance. Acceptance does not translate into approval. It requires a spirit of generosity. Allow yourself some leeway here as you practice discernment by attempting new things. Over time, you will learn to determine which satisfiers are better for you than others.

We must also remember that satisfiers are not universal. What might be a synergistic satisfier for you might not work for someone else. It is important not to manage other people's satisfiers or allow them to determine your own.

The Key to Satiation: Embodying Satisfiers

Economics, when rooted within a satiation paradigm, is a way of living devoted to embodying wealth through the practice of digesting and integrating moments of meaning. We have needs. We address these needs by digesting and integrating their associated satisfiers. Simply put, economics can be redefined as the dynamic management of your needs. This is how we bring about satiation and engender our own power of enough.

The distinction between needs and satisfiers is key. We all have similar needs, but our satisfiers are unique to us. It is by embodying meaning through exploring satisfiers that you learn how to weave together the ingredients that are specific to you. This is when you learn true self-care. Instead of adopting the next best fad to feel better about yourself, your solutions come from within. Through the practice of discernment, you refine what works and eliminate what doesn't. In this way, life becomes a testing ground where you get to be the ultimate designer of your ideal experience. Trust me, it becomes a lot of fun.

In the process, something magical occurs. As you learn to use resources more efficiently, effectively, and masterfully, you have the opportunity to develop into a more mature and creative version of yourself. Wealth becomes less about the finite game of accumulation, and more about the infinite game of exploring meaning and fulfillment. This new game of satiation is like a puzzle that involves discovering, expanding, allocating, and integrating resources to help you become the best version of yourself.

As we turn toward embodying wealth, we become curious about all types of experiences, some harder than others, for the purpose of crafting our own unique character. The amazing thing about this journey is that it does not start with a perfect picture of who we should become. Rather, it is based on the premise that we are all diamonds in the rough who just need to find our own way of polishing our shine in the world. For example, an elder is not someone we tuck away in a nursing home. Elders are people who have faced life's challenges and amassed a wealth of knowledge from the lessons they have learned. They can inspire us with everything they have experienced. The gift of understanding the power of enough is that you possess the ability to age with more wealth and well-being, regardless of your savings.

You may find that you need to focus on stabilizing your work to create a sense of abundance and security in your life. Or you might want to explore your vitality by discovering what feats your body can achieve. There may be any number of satisfiers that captivate you. The point is that wealth is founded on meaningful experiences that fulfill you. Money has a role to play. We can use it to open doors to new experiences, enabling us to find novel satisfiers that meet our needs. But it bears repeating that money cannot be your primary satisfier in life. The following practice with satisfiers will help to bring this idea home.

PRACTICE: Live Life by Design

Step 1: Choose a Need That You Would Like to Work With

Remember, needs are relatively universal, while satisfiers are unique to everyone. Select one of the human needs listed below as a doorway to invite more abundance, vitality, intimacy, and/or growth into your life. Circle the need you want to focus on.

Belonging	Participation
Connection	Physical health
Curiosity	Purpose
Financial stability	Safety
Freedom	Touch
Leisure	Understanding

Step 2: Come Up with an Example of Each Satisfier

Let's now find some satisfiers for that need. Write down an example of each type of satisfier that could fulfill the need you chose above.

Singular:

Inhibiting:

Violator:

Pseudo:

Synergistic:

Step 3: Describe Your Intention

Let's examine some of the strategies that are less likely to work. Look at what you wrote in the sections for inhibiting, violator, and pseudo satisfiers above. Briefly describe what issues might come up when you select each of these.

Notice the times in your life when you have chosen similar types of satisfiers, and describe how well that worked. This is a moment to be compassionate with yourself. Remember that while your intention was likely good, the satisfiers you picked may not have adequately addressed your needs. Take some time to write down examples of how these satisfiers negatively affected you. Be straightforward and objective. The intention here is to increase self-awareness, not to evoke shame.

Step 4: Redesign Your Life

Now that you understand how inhibiting, violating, and pseudo satisfier strategies work, see if you can redesign your life by imaging a different synergistic satisfier that might suit you better. Remember to think about what other needs might be affected when you use this strategy. Get creative and go wild. Write your ideas below. If you get stuck, talk this out with a trusted friend.

Step 5: Integrate and Apply

Now the rubber hits the road. You have full permission to try this synergistic satisfier strategy and see what happens. Pay attention to what feels different. Track the ways this satisfier allows you to integrate meaning and fulfillment into your life. Remember to think about how other needs may have been intentionally or unintentionally affected. Note the ways that other satisfiers may have gotten in the way.

You don't have to get it right; you just have to try. Life unfolds through call and response. Your body, heart, and mind will constantly signal what they need. These signals are a natural call for engagement. Yet, the shift from surviving to thriving occurs as you begin to design satisfiers that are synergistic and collaborative. Strategies that focus on these satisfiers produce an outsized impact on your life. Synergistic satisfaction has a compounding effect. Learning how to identify, practice, and refine synergistic satisfiers gives you the power to redesign your life.

Satisfiers Gone Awry

If you get stuck on this exercise, it might be helpful to have a real-life story that highlights satisfiers gone awry. Colin was a client who came to me for budgeting help. He made a good living as a resident physician, yet he was living paycheck to paycheck. He aspired to get his spending in check before any future salary increases to avoid dwindling future earnings away. He was thoroughly aware that if he didn't build a better savings muscle and spend within his means, his future financial self would suffer.

After our initial meetings and spreadsheet analysis, we discovered a couple of categories where Colin was clearly overleveraged. The amount he was spending monthly on restaurant expenses was triple what I would expect for someone living by themselves.

We dug deeper and discerned that most of Colin's restaurant expenditures were for going on dates. Colin, who had recently separated from his wife, found that dining out after work was an easy way to set up meetings with new people. The problem was that Colin felt obliged to pick up the bill, but he couldn't control what the other person ordered. There's nothing like an awkward money conversation on a first date.

Colin frequently went on first dates, occasionally on a second, but seldom progressed to a third. He wasn't building enough rapport with people to feel comfortable asking to split a check. The impact on his credit card balance was adding up. Colin was using dating to satisfy his need for connection. In this sense, the expense could be justified. However, the amount he was spending on dates was violating his need for financial stability and living within his means. One need was being actively pursued, yet it was canceling out another need in the process.

When I asked Colin why none of his dates progressed into a longer relationship that would improve his experience of connection, his first response was that he got bored easily. I had him take this question to his therapist. By our next session a week later, Colin had made a breakthrough. He realized he didn't want a long-term relationship now, but he was greatly missing the routine touch he had received in his marriage. He kept dating, trying to establish contact, but because the interactions were relatively short-lived, they didn't satisfy his pressing need for physical contact.

That aha moment helped us revise Colin's budget. We reallocated some resources for bimonthly bodywork. Colin knew of a massage therapist he had been wanting to try but thought he couldn't afford it.

When I showed him how much he'd save by dramatically decreasing his dates (as well as considering nonmonetary ways of meeting people such as going for a hike or a walk), we found a better satisfier to fulfill a more urgent need. After his first couple of massages, Colin shared how much happier he was feeling. He was receiving a quality of touch and care that was helping him heal from his recent separation, and he was giving himself the gifts of leisure and self-connection to better satisfy his immediate needs.

Colin's experience is not unique. A large part of my work with clients involves helping them identify their most pressing needs and get clear on the methods they are employing to satisfy them. We will dive deeper into working with needs in the next chapter.

For now, it is important to recognize that *how* we satisfy them is an essential component of experiencing and embodying wealth. Colin had enough resources to support himself in his relationship transition; he was simply using inadequate strategies to get there.

When I pointed out that dating, despite being a common strategy to appease the need for connection, was instead acting as a violating satisfier, we were able to find a better solution to address another need. This was crucial for Colin to achieve a better experience of well-being.

Gaining a better understanding of how satisfiers work and their impact on fulfilling one need while inhibiting or detracting from another is essential in embodying and grounding wealth. When we take the time to experiment and learn what satisfiers work for us, we use our resources in a way that truly "hits the spot." We stop consuming blindly or out of habit. Instead, consumption finds its proper place in our lives — as a means of expressing ourselves and exploring our potential.

Chapter 6 Takeaways

Choosing Intention over Reaction: This chapter underscores the importance of actively designing your life around your core values and goals, rather than passively living by the default settings you've been handed.

Embrace Needs as Pathways to Fulfillment: Needs are natural. Recognizing and embracing your human needs is a vital step toward achieving a state of embodied wealth. By accepting your needs as natural, you can establish a foundation for feeling at home within yourself, expressing your true essence, and maintaining meaningful connections with others.

Discerning Satisfiers for Compounding Wealth: The concept of "satisfiers" is critical to understanding both how we meet our needs and the strategies we employ to do so. Redesigning your life calls for a thoughtful examination of how different satisfiers affect your well-being. You can choose those that align with and enhance your overall experience of wealth and avoid the ones that detract from it.

Chapter Seven

CREATING YOUR
WEALTH MANDALA

Financial Health Is Only One Slice of the Pie

Crafting the life of your dreams involves designing your life to reflect your deepest values and personal sense of meaning. This is a pivotal step on your path toward embodying wealth. One tool you'll need to create is a *wealth mandala*, which will assist you in clarifying your needs and uncovering the most effective satisfiers for your individual journey toward well-being.

Mandala is a Sanskrit word that means "circle." This circular form represents the universe, highlighting life's infinite nature and the interconnectedness of all things. In contemporary psychology, mandalas are viewed as reflections of our individual selves, serving as tools for self-exploration and growth. We can utilize a mandala to illustrate the path of converting our suffering into joy. The mandala can help you create a framework that encompasses various facets of your being, offering fresh opportunities to explore maturity and wisdom.

Before we start our work with your wealth mandala, we need to consider the satiation paradigm in more detail. This paradigm helps to clarify two things. As you compound meaning throughout your life, you naturally create a deep well of satiation at the center of your being, which I call the power of enough. Meaning can be experienced in a diversity of ways through our three centers (mind, body, and heart).

Coming to understand satiation in this way helps us visualize how meaning accumulates at the core of our being and then becomes a resource we can draw from later. As you draw from this well of meaning at your core, you find you can lean into whatever opportunities for intimacy, growth, and vitality might arise. In this way, we can say that satiation helps us embody our own unique self-actualization.

Consider the areas in your life where finding meaning comes most naturally to you. You might also notice ways that certain areas feel less fulfilled. Observe the ebb and flow between these two cycles: the soul-oriented meaning-fulfillment cycle (body-vitality, heart-intimacy, mind-growth) and the abundance-scarcity cycle (financial stability, physical health, safety). As we turn toward the wealth mandala below, you will be given instructions on how to bring greater clarity to these differences. You can think of these cycles as making up one interconnected circuit that generates electricity (i.e., satiation). When both cycles and all three centers are being utilized, you have a profound sense of satiation and access to your source of joy.

Take a moment to visualize your own circuit as you integrate both cycles and your three centers into an expansive, energetic loop. Get a sense of where there might be a little static, places where the circuit is not fully engaged. At the same time, notice how you naturally flourish by tapping into areas of your life where meaning feels intuitively accessible. As you are about to discover, the key to igniting this energy flow lies in honoring and embracing your needs instead of disregarding them.

Bridging Our Cycles, Centers, and Needs

When we broaden our perspective beyond the abundance-scarcity cycle, we realize that security needs are only one slice of the pie. The satiation paradigm reveals other important elements for meaning, like vitality, intimacy, and growth, in addition to safety and security. Seen in this way, our well-being becomes a state of richness. True security is achieved not only through possession of scarce resources but also by connecting with the deeper sense of essence found in a wider array of needs that express our humanity.

As we move to the wealth mandala below, each center is broken down into three key needs, included alongside the three key security-oriented needs related to wealth and well-being. It is important to consider that the needs found in the body, heart, and mind centers are just as important as those found in the abundance-scarcity cycle. This was the primary contribution offered by Abraham Maslow, as discussed in the prior chapter. Our needs for self-actualization and growth are just as essential as those for security and abundance.

Within the abundance-scarcity cycle, we find the needs of financial stability, safety, and physical health. It is necessary that these are met so that we can focus our attention on the needs of the other centers. We must also remember that these security-oriented needs are never fully addressed and constantly evolving. During times of challenge or transition, these needs will naturally arise and must be addressed.

Within the body center, we discover the significance of embracing a vibrant life. Here, we can draw on the power of touch, leisure, and curiosity. Through developing these needs, we discover a basic fluidity and grace in the way we live our lives. It is important to develop these throughout one's life to ensure that a baseline of vitality is ever present.

The heart center teaches us about intimacy, guiding us through lessons in the needs of connection, belonging, and participation. It invites us to take the leap and plunge into the world of shared emotions. We can also love without that love being reciprocated. In both cases, we learn more acutely who we are through our acts of affection. We gain insight into creating emotional wealth through greater self-awareness around the innate ways we show up for ourselves and for our community.

Our mind center allows us to develop and grow as we attend to our needs for understanding, purpose, and freedom. As we explore our world through the life of the mind, we can integrate experiences and information to form wisdom and insight. Through this process, we learn to assert our individual autonomy, embracing a sense of agency and freedom within the framework of our interconnected community.

The interplay and interconnectedness of these cycles and centers give us permission to expand our focus beyond financial health. In the process, we evoke a newfound sense of security plus satiation. We tap into new resources. We uncover new strategies for nourishment and fulfillment. And we find an increased ability to embrace life as it is. The beauty of expanding our sources of wealth and deepening our acceptance of human needs is that doing so can make life fuller, simpler, yet more profound. The wealth mandala is an invitation to embody wealth by putting down the battle against having needs and embracing them as a robust pathway toward self-discovery.

• MINI MOMENT •

Which set of needs am I naturally drawn to? Why?
Which set of needs do I feel weakest in? Why?

PRACTICE: Designing Your Wealth Mandala

The wealth mandala tool can help solidify your personal commitment to a life of enough, providing you with a structured framework to chart your journey toward embodied wealth.

Below this practice, you will find descriptions of the centers and their corresponding needs. I encourage you to reflect and think through how you would personally describe each need before reading my descriptions. If you draw a blank and need inspiration, use these descriptions as a supplement to better understand what these needs mean to you. (You can find a PDF version of the wealth mandala on my website, ElizabethHusserl .com/resources, if you prefer to download and print it.)

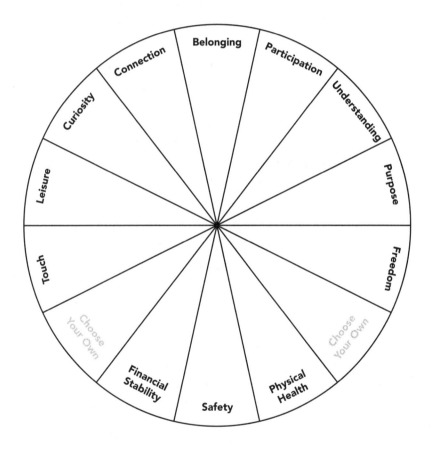

Step 1: Know Your Needs

The wealth mandala offers a visual map to chart how well you are fulfilling your needs, situating them within different cycles and centers.

- Take a moment to read the names of each of the twelve needs. In your journal, jot down a few sentences describing how you perceive each one. Give yourself plenty of time with each need and see if you can evoke examples of how this need is (or is not) present in your life.

- Notice that there are two empty places in the mandala. While I have included descriptions for three extra soul-oriented needs at the end of this chapter, feel free to choose two of those or spend some time feeling into which additional needs resonate most deeply with you. Allow yourself to intuitively sense which needs feel most alive and relevant to your journey.

- Next, connect with each need and assess your level of satisfaction using a scale of 1 to 10. A score of 1 indicates that the need is not being met at all, while a score of 10 signifies complete fulfillment in that area. Note that the goal is not to aim for perfection. There is no right way to do this, and everyone's mandala will be unique. Rather, this part of the practice will visually map where you are feeling fulfilled and where you are feeling a sense of lack.

- Near the name of each need, write down the number you assigned to it. Let yourself be as honest as possible, embracing any judgments if they arise.

Step 2: Bring Color to Your Mandala Map

- Once you have rated each need, color each section to create a visual representation of how much you feel fulfilled in that area of your life.

- For example, if you gave a particular need a 7, then color in 70 percent of that segment. Go through the entire mandala until all needs are represented. The degree to which you have shaded each slice will indicate how well you feel each need is being met.

- Bring creativity and intention to the colors you choose for each need.

Step 3: Choose Your Needs to Work With

- Now step back and observe your mandala. You can tape it to a wall or place it on your desk for easy viewing. Take a moment to reflect on the patterns and colors within the wealth mandala. What connections do you notice? What insights are revealed? Allow yourself to explore the symbolism and significance revealed in your creation.

- Immerse fully in whatever thoughts and images arise. Resist the urge to edit or filter yourself. Often, it's in facing our most challenging realizations that we uncover valuable insights.

- Then select the top two needs that are most fulfilled in your life. In your journal, write a paragraph describing the significance of having these needs met. Reflect on what's working well in these areas and how you experience fulfillment. Pay attention to any emotions that surface as you contemplate a satisfied need, even if it's not fully met. There's valuable information to be gained from understanding what is working.

- Now direct your attention to your least met needs. Take some time to journal a paragraph about each one. Explore what feels unsatisfied in these areas. Identify any obstacles you perceive that prevent you from meeting these needs. Notice the emotions that arise as you delve into this exploration. Allow yourself to acknowledge and understand the impact of these unmet needs on your well-being.

Step 4: Notice What Is Working

- Here is the interesting part. Review what you've written about the areas where you feel most satisfied.

- Now ask yourself, Are there strategies, principles, or insights that are effective for me in these areas that I can apply to the aspects of my life that need more attention? What type of satisfier am I using here?

- You might notice that qualities like confidence, support from others, or incorporating play make meeting certain needs easier than others. Alternatively, you might find yourself naturally drawn to a particular need because you find it more engaging. This prompts the question, How can you infuse more interest and appeal into the areas where you feel less fulfilled?

- Take some time to jot down any insights that come to mind, leveraging your strengths to support the areas where you require more support.

Step 5: Make a Commitment

- Finally, choose one need to focus on. It doesn't matter if it is a need that feels fulfilled that you want to enhance or a need that is weaker and needs more support.

- Decide on a period (e.g., one month) and write down three singular or synergistic satisfiers you commit to practice and engage with during that period to consciously meet this need.

- When your specified time period is complete, return to the list of satisfiers you practiced and assess the results in your journal.

Step 6: Close by Integration

- After you have journaled on these needs, close this practice with a gesture of gentle kindness to yourself. For example, you can place your hand on your heart and say, "Thank you for taking the time to explore your needs." Or you can close your eyes and imagine being showered with unconditional acceptance for everything that emerged.

- Find a safe place for your wealth mandala. You may choose to keep it visible for ongoing insights or put it away to allow time for integration. There's no right or wrong way to conclude this exercise — use it as an opportunity to discover what works best for you in meeting your needs.

- End with a deep breath, coming back to the three steps of embodying wealth — appreciation, integration, and satiation.

- Appreciate the insights you received, choose which ones you want to keep and which ones you are ready to let go of, and integrate this awareness by letting it permeate every cell of your being with the notion that you have needs, needs are natural, and you can choose the right ways to satisfy them.

Descriptions of Needs

Security-Oriented Needs

Think of security-oriented needs as the building blocks of the abundance-scarcity cycle. They're like the sturdy foundation of our well-being and sense of stability in the world. These encompass our physical, financial, and emotional safety nets, shaping how we view the resources at our disposal. When all is well in the safety department, we bask in a feeling of abundance and security, freeing us to pursue our dreams. But when these needs feel threatened or neglected, we risk getting stuck in a scarcity spiral, with fear, anxiety, and a sense of lack taking center stage.

By understanding the interplay between these needs and the abundance-scarcity cycle, we enhance our ability to foster a greater sense of resilience and prosperity in our lives.

FINANCIAL STABILITY

Financial health encompasses access to necessities such as food, shelter, and stable income, enabling us to care for our physical well-being while maintaining a secure material environment. Achieving financial stability instills a sense of confidence and equilibrium, empowering us to support ourselves and those we are responsible for.

Financial stability is also linked to our desire to have a family. The innate need to reproduce keeps us deeply connected to the material world. It can invite us to step up to the plate and take responsibility to make more money to support those we love and care about.

When challenged, financial stability takes priority, as it empowers us to create our own sense of security in the world. It is difficult to focus on leisure or curiosity when we struggle to feed our families or pay our rent. However, we must be cautious not to fixate solely on this need, especially when ample financial resources are available. As we ponder what is enough, it is crucial to address all the needs within our wealth mandala to experience embodied wealth.

STRATEGIES FOR EMBODYING FINANCIAL STABILITY

- Creating a spending, saving, and earning plan to track what comes in and what goes out.

- Aligning your spending, savings, investing, and gifting with your values and priorities.

- Accessing professional educational or financial literacy opportunities.

- Building an emergency fund to cover the unexpected bumps in the road.

- Investing in your education and skills to increase your earning potential and job stability.

- Seeking professional advice to make informed decisions about your money.

- Taking care of your physical home.

- Asking for a raise.

- Setting boundaries at work.

- Learning how to be an entrepreneur.

- Cultivating a mindset of abundance and gratitude, focusing on what you have rather than what you lack.

Safety

Safety is a core human need, encompassing both physical and emotional security. When we feel safe, we can relax and freely engage with the world, unburdened by fear or anxiety.

At its core, safety is about trust — in ourselves, others, and our environment — affording us the belief that we possess the resources and support to navigate life's challenges. This trust empowers us to forge meaningful connections, pursue aspirations, and take calculated risks for personal growth.

Safety is pivotal for experiencing abundance. When our need for safety is met, we feel grounded and secure, allowing energy to flow toward needs like creativity and connection. We are more likely to approach life from a place of openness and curiosity, rather than fear and scarcity. However, when our sense of safety is compromised, we may find ourselves stuck in a scarcity mindset. We become hypervigilant, constantly scanning our environment for potential threats and dangers. This state of chronic stress can take a toll on our physical and mental health, as well as our relationships and overall quality of life.

To nurture a sense of safety, we must address factors contributing to insecurity, including setting boundaries, fostering supportive relationships, and creating a nurturing environment. Developing inner resources like resilience and self-compassion also plays a crucial role.

Ultimately, the need for safety is a reminder of our inherent vulnerability as human beings. By honoring this need, we can create a foundation of trust that allows us to thrive and to experience abundance, joy, and fulfillment in all areas of our lives.

Strategies for Embodying Safety

- Developing a strong sense of self-compassion and self-worth to build resilience in the face of challenges.

- Cultivating self-awareness and emotional intelligence to better understand and manage our reactions to perceived threats.

- Establishing clear boundaries and communicating them assertively to others.

- Surrounding yourself with trustworthy and supportive people who contribute to your sense of security.

- Creating a physical environment that feels safe, comfortable, and nurturing.

- Getting clear on what, if anything, is making you feel unsafe.

PHYSICAL HEALTH

Maintaining physical health is fundamental to engaging fully with life and pursuing our goals. It involves caring for our bodies, preventing illness, and managing health challenges. When we make our physical well-being a priority, we establish a strong foundation for meeting other needs and fostering vitality and resilience.

Neglecting physical health can leave us depleted, vulnerable to illness, and less able to participate fully in life. It can also affect our mental and emotional well-being, creating a tangible burden that undermines our overall satisfaction and wealth.

On the other hand, when we prioritize our physical health as nonnegotiable, it has a positive ripple effect. We show up with more energy and enthusiasm, better equipped to handle challenges and enjoy life's moments. By prioritizing self-care, we set an example for others and contribute to a culture that values well-being.

As with all needs, it's important to strike a balance. Fixating on perfection can lead to stress and imbalance. Instead, view physical health as an ongoing practice that is responsive to our individual needs. By consistently making small choices that support our physical well-being, we pave the way for a life rich in vitality and embodied wealth.

Strategies for Embodying Physical Health

- Eating a balanced, nutritious diet that fuels your body and mind.

- Engaging in regular exercise and physical activity you love to maintain strength, flexibility, and endurance.

- Getting sufficient quality sleep to support your body's natural healing and rejuvenation processes.

- Managing stress through relaxation techniques, mindfulness practices, or other self-care.

- Proactively seeking preventive care and medical attention when needed to address health concerns.

Body-Oriented Needs

Body-oriented needs are integral to the vitality-energy cycle. They underscore that our bodies are not mere vessels for our minds but integral to our sense of self and interaction with the world. Through fostering touch, leisure, and curiosity, we tap into our bodies' innate wisdom, accessing a deep well of vitality, resilience, balance, and energy. Honoring these needs establishes a foundation of self-care and self-awareness, enabling fuller engagement in relationships, work, and daily life.

Touch

Touch is a cornerstone of the body center, communicating safety, connection, and trust. It's a nonverbal language that signals our presence and recognition of others. We can convey to someone else through our body center that we are here for them, and they are fully seen. Whether it's a warm hug or the sensation of wind on our skin, touch taps directly into our vitality and connects us to the energy around us.

Our skin, which is our largest organ, acts as a gateway to our physical realm. Satisfying touch, like a heartfelt embrace, triggers the release of oxytocin, a hormone that fosters trust, strengthens bonds, reduces anxiety, and motivates us to act in the spirit of generosity. Touch isn't limited to human contact; it extends to our interactions with the world around us, grounding us in our surroundings. We "touch" the elements when we feel water on our skin or wind on our face, or walk barefoot on the ground and jump into a pool on a hot day.

Transparency accompanies touch, allowing us to embrace our imperfections and share our full selves. Through trust, we dismantle barriers and invite others to witness our authenticity. While navigating differences in touch can be challenging, it's integral to our self-discovery journey. We are forced to do the harder work of facing our fears and letting other people into our lives.

Touch invites courage, facilitating connections between our centers. It enables our minds to delve into emotions and teaches our bodies to surrender and feel held by the heart. Despite its complexities, touch reveals layers of our identity, fostering a sense of safety and belonging. When a baby falls asleep on a caregiver's chest, its body can learn to surrender and experience being held.

Touch is not always easy. It invites a diversity of opinions, different ways of being, and personal beliefs that we sometimes cling to as ultimate truths. It requires consent, making it a tricky domain to explore, and we can feel burdened by social, cultural, and religious norms. Navigating differences in touch can be uncomfortable and may even be seen as inappropriate to others at times.

Yet, when we find the courage to explore the quality and style of touch that most nourishes our bodies, we invite a different way of knowing both ourselves and the physical world. Despite its edges, touch is an essential component of peeling back the onion and revealing who we are. Our hearts and minds can only take us so far. There will always be more layers of ourselves to reveal. This requires the use of touch to establish a physical sense of safety and belonging in our lives. As we get to the all-important core of being, we discover who we really are.

The true test of touch can be found in moments when we experience a feeling of profound awe and presence. This is the sense of being available, seen, felt, and heard. We are *in touch* with both ourselves and the world around us. Time ceases to exist. Instead, we inhabit an overwhelming knowing that everything is OK just as it is. In this sense, touch supports a deeper experience of safety and security. When we feel more secure, we loosen our grip on money, external expectations, and material things.

STRATEGIES FOR EMBODYING TOUCH

- Engaging in regular physical affection with loved ones, such as hugs, cuddles, or hand-holding.

- Exploring what types of touch feel good to you and what types do not.

- Practicing consent with others.

- Practicing self-care techniques to release tension and promote relaxation.

- Exploring different types of touch-based practices, such as acupuncture, craniosacral therapy, or reflexology.

- Being mindful of your physical boundaries and communicating them clearly to others.

- Cultivating a sense of comfort and acceptance with your own body through self-care and positive self-talk.

LEISURE

Believe it or not, the need for leisure is fundamental. If work is the inhale, leisure is the exhale — a vital release that replenishes our energy and recognizes that times of "doing nothing" are essential for our overall health and wealth.

Leisure reminds us to be present and right where we are, to relax and rediscover the joy of daydreaming, playing, and embracing free time. In this state of idleness, we nurture curiosity, receptivity, and imagination. Instead of constantly doing more, we learn to appreciate the value of doing less, prioritizing quality over quantity.

Meeting our need for leisure is crucial for our overall vitality and enjoyment of life. Just as a personal trainer emphasizes the importance of muscle recovery for physical health, leisure allows us to recharge and rebuild stamina. It's a chance to redefine creativity and success by stepping away from societal pressures and reconnecting with our true selves.

Through leisure, we explore new dimensions of thought and experience, finding solace in silence and stillness. Daydreaming becomes a bridge to fresh insights and perspectives, enriching our understanding of the world. Leisure reminds us that we are enough as we are, without the constant pressure to achieve or improve.

By honoring our need for leisure, we nourish our vitality and replenish our well of life. We remember that we are good enough just the way we are. We embrace a slower pace, allowing ourselves to simply be without the need for constant productivity and overdoing. In doing so, we find ourselves more alive, content, and at peace. We feel replenished and well nourished.

STRATEGIES FOR EMBODYING LEISURE

- Blocking off time in your calendar to do nothing.

- Dedicating time for leisure activities that bring you joy and relaxation.

- Exploring new hobbies or interests that engage you in fun, playful, or creative ways.

- Practicing mindfulness or meditation to cultivate a sense of presence and enjoyment in the moment.

- Prioritizing social connections and shared experiences with friends and loved ones.

- Maintaining a healthy work-life balance that allows for sufficient rest, relaxation, and recreation.

- Letting go of the fear of missing out, and practicing saying no when you need time to replenish.

- Savoring stillness.

- Being out in nature, letting yourself be an essential part of the natural world.

CURIOSITY

Curiosity is the spark that ignites our desire to understand and explore the world around us. It draws us toward what fascinates us, guiding us to our purpose and helping us reach our full potential. As we hone new skills, knowledge, and experiences, curiosity becomes the driving force behind our growth and development.

At its core, curiosity is intrinsic to our nature. Just observe a young child immersed in play and discovery — they eagerly explore, touch, taste, and study their surroundings, driven by an insatiable thirst for knowledge. This innate curiosity not only shapes our understanding of the world but also fosters happiness, confidence, and self-esteem.

The neuropsychologist Rick Hanson considers learning to be one of the most essential skills needed to foster personal development and growth, calling it the "superpower of superpowers."

Learning is not just about acquiring data and information that can breed good habits, strengths, and skills. It can also identify strategies that help us heal.

When we embrace curiosity as a transformative force, we unlock the power of embodied learning, which in turn nurtures our bodies, hearts, and minds. This approach fosters creativity, innovation, and resilience. By embracing curiosity as a fundamental need, it becomes a powerful catalyst for collecting and gathering resources for a life of embodied wealth.

STRATEGIES FOR EMBODYING CURIOSITY

- Cultivating a beginner's mind and approaching new experiences with openness and wonder.

- Asking questions and seeking out new knowledge or perspectives on topics that interest you.

- Traveling to new places or immersing yourself in different cultures to broaden your horizons.

- Engaging in lifelong learning through courses, workshops, or self-study.

- Surrounding yourself with diverse and stimulating people, ideas, and experiences that challenge and inspire you.

Heart-Oriented Needs

The heart-oriented needs are vital aspects of human existence that shape our relationships, our sense of self, and our place in the world. Nestled within the intimacy-vulnerability cycle, these needs stem from a deep longing for authentic connections with others, rooted in vulnerability and openness. As we move through stages of connection, belonging, and participation, we deepen our capacity for intimacy, each stage building on the last. Embracing these heart-oriented needs enhances our lives with profound experiences, fostering growth, healing, and personal transformation.

CONNECTION

Connection serves as the bedrock of intimacy, initiating the bond that draws us closer to others and fosters a sense of closeness. It is the profound feeling of being seen, heard, and valued, recognizing a shared connection with another individual. Built through shared experiences, interests, or values, connection thrives on open communication, empathy, and vulnerability.

In the early stages of any relationship, connection is the driving force, sparking excitement and joy in discovering someone new. It's the foundation on which deeper intimacy is built, creating a space of trust and safety where we can reveal our true selves. Yet while connection is vital, it's only the starting point. Sustaining meaningful relationships requires a willingness to explore our own complexities and truly accept others for who they are.

Humans are wired for bonding; without healthy connections, we risk emotional and physical distress, leading to harmful coping mechanisms. If we live in an environment of isolation, desperation, and lovelessness, our addictions find a fertile ground, and we look to bond with something that will give us a sense of relief. That might be gambling, drugs, work, sex, or overspending.

A recent client shared that his manager at work gave him one goal for the next quarter: to prioritize creating a meaningful relationship with at least one person in the department. The request floored my client. Creating connections was not in his job description as a tech researcher. Yet as he sat with it, he recognized that his manager could see he was not happy at work. He was great at what he did, but he lacked a sense of belonging and meaning.

Though hesitant at first, he realized the potential for wealth and meaning in embracing connection. He accepted that underneath his resistance was vulnerability and fear. He had a rocky relationship with his father and did not trust that people could simply love and appreciate him for who he was. Despite feeling vulnerable and afraid of rejection, he discovered the courage and vitality to acknowledge his need for connection and took the risk of doing so.

Acknowledging our need for connection requires both humility and bravery, as it opens us to the risk of not being loved in return. But by extending our capacity to connect deeply — with ourselves, others, and the world — we deepen our emotional health and find true wealth in the bonds we form.

STRATEGIES FOR EMBODYING CONNECTION

- Prioritizing quality time and presence with loved ones, free from distractions or interruptions.

- Expressing gratitude and appreciation for the people in your life through your word and your actions.

- Practicing vulnerability and openness in your relationships, sharing your thoughts, feelings, and experiences authentically.

- Seeking out opportunities for meaningful conversations and interactions with others.

- Cultivating a sense of connection with nature and the world around you through outdoor activities or mindfulness practices.

BELONGING

As we cultivate a sense of connection with others, we discover a deeper level of intimacy called belonging. Belonging entails feeling part of something larger, where we are accepted and appreciated for our true selves, free from any fear of being judged or excluded. Belonging empowers us to take risks, be vulnerable, and explore our inner selves. In a community where we belong, we feel secure, knowing we're supported by people who embrace us unconditionally.

Belonging is a deeper form of intimacy than connection, as it requires a greater level of trust, vulnerability, and commitment. It is about more than finding common ground or sharing experiences. It is about forging a shared sense of identity and purpose. When we belong, we become part of a collective narrative that infuses our lives with meaning and direction.

Belonging fuels communal wealth, enabling us to thrive personally and professionally. It allows us to contribute authentically, stepping into roles and leadership positions with integrity and a sense of duty to others. As collaboration flourishes, collective efforts surpass individual contributions.

Imagine a world that values belonging above material possessions. Here, our focus shifts from accumulation to growth and development. Belonging anchors us, providing a profound sense of safety and grounding. The more we nurture this human need, the more rooted we feel in both ourselves and our lives.

Strategies for Embodying Belonging

- Seeking out communities or groups that share your values, interests, or experiences.

- Cultivating a strong sense of self-identity and authenticity in your interactions with others.

- Practicing active listening and empathy to build deeper, more meaningful connections.

- Volunteering or contributing to causes that align with your passions and values.

- Nurturing a sense of belonging within yourself through self-acceptance and compassion.

PARTICIPATION

As we engage with others, we discover another profound expression of intimacy: participation. Participation is actively engaging with others and the world, using our unique talents to contribute to something greater. It's about cocreating, feeling purposeful, and being part of a larger narrative unfolding around us.

Participation requires trust and belonging, as it involves taking risks and stepping into discomfort. It's not passive; it's about shaping and influencing our surroundings. By using our voices, skills, and passions, we add beauty and make a meaningful impact. This level of intimacy combines connection, belonging, agency, and purpose. Through our participation, we contribute to the growth of our communities and reciprocate love and support. We don't just find our place; we help shape it.

Participation marks the deepest intimacy, where we feel fully acknowledged, valued, and empowered. It's an important part of the journey from connection to belonging, leading to a life filled with purpose and fulfillment.

Contrary to popular belief, we don't need to know our purpose to participate. Through engagement and participation, purpose reveals itself. Participation exposes us to life's mysteries, opening doors of synchronicity and revealing our true calling. Participation brings moments of profound meaning. Whether it's a deep connection, time spent in nature, or a joyful dance, these experiences align us with our purpose.

For me personally, participation shows up whenever I turn to my husband and say with a smile, "I love my life!" It could happen after making a meaningful connection, going on a bike ride in nature, attending a lively dance party, or having a profound meeting with a client. In those moments, what's important is not what I just did, but rather the feeling I obtained by fully participating in my life. It is by participating that I have found my purpose. The sheer act of engaging with life fills us up, until one day we wake up recognizing our worth and embracing the fact that our cups are full.

STRATEGIES FOR EMBODYING PARTICIPATION

- Keenly paying attention to what creates satisfaction and moments of meaning for you.

- Actively engaging in your communities through volunteering, attending or hosting events, or joining organizations.

- Saying yes to spontaneous opportunities that arise and feel aligned.

- Speaking up for causes or issues that matter to you, even when uncomfortable.

- Contributing your unique skills, talents, or perspectives to group projects or initiatives.

- Taking a risk and offering something new.

- Practicing active citizenship by staying informed, voting, and taking part in the democratic process.

- Cultivating a sense of agency and empowerment in your ability to make a difference in the world around you.

Mind-Oriented Needs

The mind-oriented needs are vital for our growth and development. They shape our intellectual, psychological, and spiritual evolution and reflect the fact that our minds are dynamic, constantly adapting to life's challenges. By nurturing the needs of understanding, purpose, and freedom, we unlock our mind's potential, tapping into wisdom, creativity, and resilience. Honoring these needs establishes a foundation of self-awareness, reflection, and determination, which empowers us to navigate life's complexities with confidence and clarity.

UNDERSTANDING

Understanding is more than just accumulating facts. It's about processing, interpreting, and applying knowledge meaningfully. True understanding brings clarity and mastery, enabling us to navigate complexities and make decisions that align with our values.

Think of understanding as the clarity amid the chaos of information overload. Much like navigating a subway system in a new city, it's not only about knowing the signs, but also about gaining confidence in the direction you are heading. It's about digesting data to meet your individual needs.

Delving deeper, understanding becomes the bedrock of wisdom, fostering critical thinking and insight. It reveals the interconnectedness of ideas, guiding our actions with grace and resilience. Deep understanding of ourselves and the world equips us to tackle life's challenges.

Cultivating understanding requires a commitment to lifelong learning and a willingness to challenge our assumptions. It entails honing critical thinking, seeking diverse perspectives, and reflecting deeply. Through this continual expansion of understanding, we embrace new possibilities and continue to evolve.

STRATEGIES FOR EMBODYING UNDERSTANDING

- Practicing active listening. When engaging with others, make a conscious effort to fully listen and understand their perspectives without judgment or interruption.

- Seeking out diverse viewpoints. Expose yourself to a wide range of ideas, cultures, and experiences to broaden your understanding of the world.

- Engaging in self-reflection. Take time to regularly reflect on your thoughts, feelings, and experiences, and look for patterns and insights that can deepen your self-understanding.

- Asking questions and seeking clarification. When faced with new or complex information, don't be afraid to ask questions and seek further explanation until you feel a sense of clarity.

- Applying your knowledge in real-world situations. Look for opportunities to put your understanding into practice, whether through problem-solving, decision-making, or creative pursuits. This will help you refine and deepen your understanding over time.

Purpose

Purpose is our compass in life, guiding us toward our personal growth and our understanding of our place in the world. Our purpose points to our unique expression, which is intertwined with how we experience ourselves in relation to our surroundings.

Being human is hard. Without a clear sense of purpose, we're adrift, lacking internal guideposts for self-worth and identity. This can lead to jealousy, depression, or feeling overwhelmed by choices, ultimately eroding our sense of self. When we don't know ourselves, we can mistakenly replace personal identity with a herd mentality. Or we can have so many options available we feel overwhelmed and paralyzed. The more we are aware of the ingredients that make up who we are and what is important to us, the more skilled we get at navigating the intricacies of life.

Our purpose evolves as we do, requiring that we shed identities that no longer serve us. This journey involves letting go of attachments and allowing our true selves to emerge. It's a stage that often accompanies the process of individuation, which can bring confusion, anger, or grief but is necessary for growth. We must be willing to let go of our identity as we pass through various stages in our lives.

Bill Plotkin, one of my favorite psychologists, suggests that the journey from adolescence to adulthood is a rite of passage. Adulthood does not come simply with age. It is not achieved with a certain job, status, or title. Instead, it requires letting go of old stories and allowing the hidden layers of our souls to shine through. That is the point at which we commit to embodying our soul's calling for the benefit of all beings. As we embody our purpose in this way, we truly become adults.

The journey to self-discovery isn't straightforward; there's no instruction manual to follow. However, despite being nonlinear, it's incredibly valuable. A solid sense of self-identity serves as a compass, guiding our decisions. It empowers us to navigate complex situations by tapping into the wisdom of all aspects of ourselves, not just our minds.

Fulfilling our purpose isn't just an individual endeavor; it's a collective journey of discovering how we can contribute to others and the world. This requires openness to diverse expressions and perspectives, fostering a culture that embraces and encourages individual identities within the community.

STRATEGIES FOR EMBODYING PURPOSE

- Reflecting on your passions, values, and strengths to identify areas of your life that feel most meaningful and fulfilling.

- Connecting the dots between moments of meaning to see what themes, patterns, and insights arise.

- Setting clear, actionable goals that align with your sense of purpose and direction.

- Seeking out opportunities to use your skills and talents in service of something greater than yourself.

- Asking for reflections from others on how they experience you. Listening for what themes emerge.

- Cultivating a growth mindset and embracing challenges as opportunities for learning and development.

- Regularly reassessing and adjusting your priorities and actions to ensure alignment with your sense of purpose.

- Cultivating practices to help you trust that you are on track.

- Keeping a satiation journal, which will be introduced in the next chapter.

- Asking for encouragement and support often. This is a sign of strength and courage.

FREEDOM

Freedom, in its purest sense, is the ability to act, think, and be true to ourselves. When we are free, we express ourselves without reservation. It fuels creativity, novelty, original thinking, productivity, and a better quality of life. When we lack freedom, the value of our material possessions diminishes. As our wealth loses its luster, it cannot be utilized to express our true selves.

The value of freedom extends beyond personal expression. It's a cornerstone of modern society, protected by rights such as freedom of speech, religion, and assembly. With each of these rights, we safeguard the basic right to be ourselves. The threat of losing our freedom can even motivate us to sacrifice our lives.

Yet true freedom isn't solitary and doesn't occur in a vacuum. True freedom is experienced within a community. It's not about asserting our self-righteousness but about recognizing the impact of our actions on others. Being truly free means finding a balance between individuality and communal responsibility.

When we integrate personal freedom with understanding and participation, we create an inclusive environment where diverse expressions are welcomed. We are aware of the distinct impact that our expressions have on the greater world. This collective freedom isn't about self-importance. It is about creating spaces where we can thrive, trusting there is enough freedom to go around.

STRATEGIES FOR EMBODYING FREEDOM

- Cultivating a strong sense of autonomy, personal agency, and choice in your thoughts, feelings, and actions.

- Respecting the autonomy of others with the same kindness you would offer yourself.

- Setting healthy boundaries and learning to say no to commitments or expectations that don't align with your values.

- Exploring new ideas, perspectives, or ways of being that challenge your assumptions or limiting beliefs.

- Taking responsibility for your feelings of discomfort if your sense of freedom rubs up against someone else's.

- Practicing flexibility without losing yourself.

- Prioritizing self-care and self-compassion as a foundation for authentic self-expression.

- Advocating for social, political, or economic freedoms that promote equity and justice for all.

Soul-Centered Needs

Exploring the depths of our being and our needs unveils new pathways to fulfillment. This section provides some examples of other needs you can add to your wealth mandala. There are several human needs that could be included here, but for me, three are of particular interest: creativity, service, and transcendence.

As you begin to inhabit the depths of vitality found through your body center, the more soul-centric need of creativity starts to arise. Similarly, intimacy found through the heart center gives way to service, while growth developed through the mind center takes on a flavor of transcendence. These needs resonate deeply with our souls, reflecting our yearning for connection to something greater. They remind us that life is more than mere happenstance; it's infused with purpose and significance beyond ourselves.

Through nurturing creativity, seeking transcendence, and embracing service, we unlock the profound potential of our souls. These endeavors inspire us, instill awe, and foster compassion, enriching not only our lives but also the lives of others. By honoring these soul-centered needs, we establish a bedrock of authenticity, unity, and meaning, paving the way for a life imbued with purpose and fulfillment. We'll delve into each of these needs, exploring their transformative power and their role in fostering spiritual growth and harmony.

CREATIVITY

Creativity is the spark that ignites our capacity to innovate and invent. It beckons us to build, design, and imagine, allowing our passions and intuition to find new forms of expression. Born out of the vitality of the body center, creativity fuels our engagement with the world, driving us to move beyond financial stability and embrace the daring pursuit of novelty, innovation, and self-expression.

Yet expressing our imaginations demands courage. It requires us to divert our vitality toward birthing something new, risking failure and discomfort in the process.

There's a boldness required for creativity. It is inherently connected to agency. It takes courage to redirect our vitality away from meeting our material sustenance and channel it toward birthing something new that may not necessarily meet a material need.

When stifled, creativity festers as unfulfilled yearning or misguided beliefs that it must yield tangible or productive results to be valid. However, discomfort is an integral part of the creative journey, revealing our deepest desires and urging us to confront our fears. Embracing this discomfort allows us to tap into our potential and give voice to our innermost feelings. It challenges us to pay attention, summon courage, and cultivate the discipline needed to navigate creative resistance.

As Julia Cameron, author of *The Artist's Way*, writes, "We often resist what we need most." Our profound sense of restlessness and longing sheds important light on how we can leave an imprint in this world. Creativity serves up our potentiality on a silver platter. We need to learn how to pay attention and find the courage, discipline, and spaciousness to face the resistance and invite creativity to come through. In the crucible of creative discomfort lies the journey toward full expression and satiation.

STRATEGIES FOR EMBODYING CREATIVITY

- Setting aside dedicated time and space for creative pursuits, free from distractions or interruptions.

- Exploring new artistic mediums, techniques, or styles to expand your creative repertoire.

- Taking risks and learning from what didn't go quite right in the past.

- Collaborating with others on creative projects or initiatives to spark new ideas and perspectives.

- Practicing mindfulness or meditation to cultivate a sense of presence and flow in your creative process.

- Seeking out opportunities to share your creative work with others through exhibitions, performances, or online platforms.

- Being creative for creativity's sake, with no outcome in mind.

SERVICE

Service naturally arises from our heart center as we discover the possibilities and joys of intimacy with others. Our natural turn toward service embodies our innate urge to contribute to something greater than ourselves, leveraging our skills, talents, and resources for the betterment of the world. It signifies a quest to extend beyond personal gain and find fulfillment by making a positive impact.

Engaging in acts of service transcends mere activity. Service is not about being busy. Rather, it evokes a profound sense of fulfillment and connection to a larger purpose. Through service, we forge bonds with our community and experience a deep-seated belonging that nourishes our souls.

Service manifests in many forms, from local volunteering to careers aligned with our values. It can involve acts of kindness and generosity, such as helping a neighbor in need or donating to a cause we believe in. It can also involve using our unique talents and abilities to create something of value for others, whether that be a work of art, an invention, or a solution to a pressing social problem.

Nurturing a spirit of service is akin to a spirit of generosity. It helps us to move beyond our self-centered concerns and connect with the larger web of life. Yet the pursuit of service is not always easy. It requires us to step outside our comfort zones and confront obstacles. It also demands that we cultivate a sense of humility and openness, recognizing that we have much to learn from others, and that our contributions, however small, can make a difference.

Ultimately, service offers transformative rewards, infusing our lives with purpose and meaning. By integrating acts of service into our daily lives, we cultivate connection, compassion, and wisdom, improving both our existence and the lives of those around us.

STRATEGIES FOR EMBODYING SERVICE

- Finding causes or issues that align with your passions and values.

- Seeking opportunities to contribute your time, skills, or resources.

- Practicing random acts of kindness or generosity toward others, without the expectation of recognition or rewards.

- Cultivating a sense of empathy and compassion for those who are suffering or in need.

- Discovering opportunities for leadership or mentorship and using your skills and experience to guide and support others.

- Embracing a mindset of humility and recognizing that your individual actions are part of a larger web of interconnectedness and interdependence.

TRANSCENDENCE

Transcendence is the journey of moving beyond the confines of our individual selves. This impulse takes us beyond our individual minds and our personal growth as we seek connection with something greater. It beckons us to discover meaning and purpose outside our personal desires, fostering unity with the world around us.

Through spiritual practices, contemplation, or immersion in nature, we embark on pathways to transcendence. These endeavors often evoke feelings of awe, wonder, and interconnectedness, shifting our perspective and illuminating our place in the larger scheme of things and the grand tapestry of our existence.

Nurturing transcendence is vital for our holistic well-being. It liberates us from the constraints of ego-driven desires, offering profound peace, contentment, and alignment with our true essence.

Yet the pursuit of transcendence is not always easy. It requires confronting our fears, doubts, and attachments to the material world, cultivating humility and openness along the way.

Nevertheless, embracing transcendence can be deeply transformative, infusing our lives with purpose and meaning. By integrating practices that facilitate transcendence into our daily lives, we foster connection, compassion, and wisdom, enhancing not only our own existence but also the lives of those around us.

Strategies for Embodying Transcendence

- Engaging in regular spiritual or contemplative practices, such as prayer, meditation, or yoga.

- Seeking out experiences of awe and wonder in nature, art, or other sources of inspiration.

- Exploring different philosophical or spiritual traditions to gain new insights into the nature of reality and your place in it.

- Cultivating a sense of connection and unity with something greater than yourself, whether through religion, spirituality, or personal belief.

- Spending unstructured time in nature.

- Practicing compassion, empathy, and loving-kindness toward yourself and others as a pathway to transcendence.

Chapter 7 Takeaways

Creating Your Wealth Mandala: This transformative practice helps us navigate toward a wider and personalized definition of wealth that goes beyond financial health. It is a tool for self-discovery and growth. By visualizing your life as a mandala, you can explore your personal journey toward wealth and well-being. The mandala represents the universe and the interconnectedness of life, underscoring the idea that personal growth involves acknowledging and integrating various aspects of your existence.

Wealth Is Multidimensional: Wealth is about more than financial resources. It encompasses two distinct cycles: abundance-scarcity and meaning-fulfillment. In the framework of the meaning-fulfillment cycle, each center (body, heart, and mind) has three distinct needs. Each dimension has its own set of needs and corresponds to different aspects of life — security (financial stability, safety, and physical health); body (touch, leisure, and curiosity); heart (connection, belonging, and participation); and mind (understanding, purpose, and freedom). As you discover new depths of meaning in these four centers, you can also discover more soul-oriented needs: creativity (body), service (heart), and transcendence (mind). Recognizing and nurturing each need can lead to a richer, more balanced sense of wealth.

Addressing and Embracing Needs: Embodied wealth requires the recognition of needs and how they are met across different areas of your life. Security-oriented needs are foundational, but they are only part of a larger picture that includes the needs of the body, heart, and mind. By addressing these needs, you can build a more comprehensive and fulfilling life. And as you develop your ability to integrate the meaning in your life, new soul-oriented needs become important (for example, creativity, service, and transcendence).

Chapter Eight

WHAT IS ENOUGH?

Redefining Success as Satiation

When I was a young girl, my mom encouraged me to use the phrase "I feel satisfied!" after a meal I enjoyed, instead of saying "I feel full!" Manners aside, she was teaching me a fundamental lesson that underlies everything I offer in this book: There is a difference between feeling full and feeling satisfied.

Fullness generally refers to a physical sensation of having filled one's stomach. It's the bodily response to the volume of food consumed, which contributes to the feeling of having no desire to continue eating. Fullness is more about the actual physical state of being after consuming food. Eating to the point of being full addresses the abundance-scarcity cycle — we required food to fulfill one of our needs. Once you eat to the point of being full, eating more no longer fulfills a need but exceeds it. Overeating doesn't make you any less hungry, nor does it add to a sense of wealth. In fact, in some extreme cases, overeating can be a violating satisfier. We eat to meet a need, but if this leads to us becoming overweight, a whole host of other health concerns might arise.

Satiation, while related to fullness, has a broader psychological component. It is the process that causes one to stop eating, which includes the feeling of being satisfied. Unlike fullness, which can occur simply because there is no more room for food, satiation is influenced by the types of food eaten, the enjoyment of the meal, taste, and smell. It signals not just the cessation of eating but the satisfaction derived from the meal, which can prevent further eating until hunger returns.

Satisfaction is a guiding principle that steers our journey, not just an end. The very notion of satiation is rooted in the Latin *satis*, which suggests the state of being satisfied. Satiation is not a static end point but a transformative experience. Satiation brings a radical shift; it is what motivates you. We can never get rid of our innate drive and desire to seek. But as we learn to embody and compound moments of meaning, we develop direct access to our power of enough to build wealth from the inside out.

Here's the hidden truth of the abundance-scarcity cycle: aiming for fullness can tip the scales from abundance into indulgence, hindering one's sense of well-being instead of adding to it. Feeling like we have an abundance of food can help us to feel secure, but consuming too much does not do anything more to address our hunger.

You can become full from practically anything: water, food, activities, work, deadlines, people you love. But being full of something doesn't mean we are satisfied. And adding more resources or experiences to an already full plate does not necessarily bring about satiation. To embody satiation, we need to digest and integrate the meaningful experiences in our lives.

As you move beyond just meeting your security needs like financial and physical health, you pursue deeper desires that engage you fully with life. Our desires have a role to play, teaching us about our needs. They are not merely indicators of lack. They propel us toward growth by revealing ways to satisfy ourselves. We long for wholeness. If channeled correctly, desires can propel us out of a narrow focus on the abundance-scarcity cycle into the bigger continuum of meaning and completeness. Remember that we are wired to seek, but we can turn and redirect desires toward meaning and purpose. When we embody these, we can experience the world feeling nourished and satisfied, rather than simply full.

This proactive stance empowers us to shift toward a richer, purpose-filled narrative where we each have the power to design our life. The ancient Greeks called this new way of relating to the world *eudaimonia*, which translates to "human flourishing." Eudaimonia stems not from lack but from a drive toward fulfillment. True embodied wealth encourages you to dive deep into the infinite well of meaning within you — embracing your power of enough.

Often when I practice digesting an experience to create a sense of satiation, I close my eyes. This helps me filter out the external world and focus on what is bringing me satisfaction at the moment. The more I pay attention, the more satisfaction expands, and the more meaning I can integrate.

This process brings us to a place of trust — a knowing in our bodies that we can take care of ourselves with what we choose and what we have. The quality of how and what we pick matters. Are you chasing after quantity and packing your days with too many commitments and things? Or are you practicing quality, taking the time and effort to discern what strategies work best to fit your needs and leave you feeling satisfied? These are crucial questions to ask for moving from a paradigm of accumulating wealth to one of embodying it.

• MINI MOMENT •

Where in my life do I feel truly satisfied? What am I doing? Who am I with? Where am I?

My initial experience with satiation came after teaching one of my first workshops. It had been a great day — not only had people shown up, but they also fully participated. Through their stories, they shared how shame and anxiety were part of their experiences with money, regardless of how much they had in the bank.

One woman described how receiving family support was incredibly useful, but it kept her in a cycle of guilt and shame. She struggled to feel that she deserved the help. Another participant lived in an entirely different reality, yet she shared a similar sentiment. For the life of her, she couldn't figure out how to break the cycle of living paycheck to paycheck. Like the other participant, she felt ashamed, but it had a different flavor. Both participants assumed that money symbolized success, and because they were not financially independent, they both felt like failures.

Both women felt stuck with a profound sense of lack. What had started as a natural drive to be successful turned into desperation and shame. I led them through a meditation with their centers — body, heart, and mind — and asked them to tap into what had satisfied them in their journey thus far. One woman tapped into a sense of perseverance and grit she didn't know she had. The other woman recognized how exhausted she felt from pushing away the family support. When she relaxed that habit, she could embody a sense of agency in how she designed her life.

Their notions of success shifted to how they were actively participating in life, rather than how much money they had in their bank accounts. These simple shifts had a profound impact. By redefining success to focus on their experiences of satiation, they identified a wider array of resources.

As I sat at the table after the workshop, I noticed that I was swallowing. I wasn't eating anything, so this caught me by surprise. I realized that my body was using the act of swallowing to digest the impactful experiences I had encountered.

Trusting that my body was on to something, I intentionally paused and swallowed again. As I did this, I started to understand how powerful it was to ingest the moments of meaning that had come from the experiences I'd had that day. It was only in looking back that I could recognize this life-changing experience for what it was.

As I sat at my kitchen table that evening, I had one of my first conscious encounters with embodying wealth and experiencing the power of enough. All I knew at the moment was that my body wanted to celebrate how much the workshop had affected me in profound and positive ways.

I had known for years how important it was to celebrate important moments, but this act of swallowing felt different. I was allowing myself to *consume* my experience and communicate to my cells what had happened and how it had changed me. I felt time expand as I realized that *I was enough*.

At that moment, it didn't matter how many people had been at the workshop. It was irrelevant that I had only covered half the material I had planned, or that one exercise completely flopped. What mattered was that the experience of my day was full of opportunities for insight, shared connections, and meaning. And because I had taken the time to appreciate this fact, the day had become immensely transformational. I had been available to the curiosity, confusion, and laughter in the room. I recognized that I had created a container of safety and connection for the participants, and in doing so, I had affected their lives in powerful ways.

When I swallowed, I remember thinking, What if we consumed meaning like this every day? What if we gave ourselves permission to digest and integrate the meaningful moments that occurred so often in our lives? What if this was what I had been looking for? Was this a whole new way of nourishing ourselves and building wealth? It would be a different form of consumption from eating, but perhaps one that would satisfy us to our core.

At a primal level, we look for things to fill us up, whether it's food, clothes, relationships, or social media. But in the deepest part of ourselves, we are not hungry for material resources such as food. We long to be filled by meaningful experiences, like new ideas and connections with others and the world around us. Some of us crave exhilaration, others yearn for stillness. Some cherish connection and insight. If we are going to experience satiation, we must figure out what need is asking to be fulfilled and how best to satisfy it. This is not always easy. We can misread our needs, and unfortunately, fulfilling the wrong need may make us feel full, sluggish, or hungry for more.

Our day-to-day consumption allows us to survive, but meaningful consumption enables us to thrive. When we move from basic survival to a state of flourishing, we create more meaning in our lives. As we begin to equate success with satiation, the act of consuming becomes a fertile ground of choice, agency, and nourishment.

This sounds good, but how do you do it? By taking one step beyond the collective wisdom created by celebrating your successes and acknowledging your failures. As you do this, you start living from a place of satiation, rather than one of scarcity and lack. As you turn toward what inspires you, what fills you up is naturally revealed. And as you eliminate what doesn't serve you, you digest the meaning you've experienced, allowing yourself to compound it and find satiation.

> ### • MINI MOMENT •
>
> *Connect success to satiation. Let that possibility sink in. Close your eyes and breathe. Now, open them and describe what satisfaction feels like when it has permission to fill you to your core.*

The Art of Curated Meaning

A client of mine was immobile for several weeks with multiple foot injuries. As she sat on her couch, recovering, she had ample time to reflect on and admire the impressive art wall she had just created with photographs from her life. I asked her about her experience of taking in her visual memories. She shared, "In my moments of quiet, I realized I wasn't hungry for more. I was hungry for depth. By being forced to do nothing, I came to realize I can access depth by taking the time to reflect and surround myself with the things that I care about and by curating my life experiences, my home, and my friends. It's the act of right editing that makes our lives a work of art."

Like it did with my client, satiation takes us beyond feeling grateful for our lives, toward a more skilled understanding of who we are and what satisfies us to the core. It can help pinpoint our human needs more precisely, along with the nuanced differences between them, and identify the most effective approaches to meet them.

It is from this place that we begin to live our lives with the power of enough. A path of enoughness is not about arriving somewhere. It is not our list of accomplishments that defines or describes us, nor the sum of our successes. It is not even about understanding the nuances that make up our relationship to money, or feeling that we have our money life totally figured out.

A life of enoughness is based on a practice of satiation whereby we lean into the moments of meaning in our lives. It is about ensuring that we have the resources to meet our everyday needs, no matter what we face. It asks us to take the step from quantity to quality by focusing on growth and personal development. But in the end, it is mostly about appreciating the meaning in our lives.

When we recognize we have the agency to develop our own strategies of well-being, our ability to create wealth expands beyond our wildest dreams. Satiation and the power of enough remain present in our lives well past the fleeting moments of happiness and success.

The Key to Satiation:
Integrating Satisfiers and Centers

In chapter 1, you learned three simple steps for embodying wealth. First, *recognize* and *appreciate* each moment of meaning that nourishes you. Second, *digest* these moments of meaning by *integrating* what nourishes you and *releasing* whatever your body doesn't need. And third, allow these moments of meaning to accumulate and *compound*, creating a sense of *satiation* that connects you to your own unique expression of the power of enough. Now, let's dive into examples of how this process works in each center.

In the body, satiation manifests as moments of vitality as needs like touch, leisure, and curiosity are met. When you recognize and appreciate nourishing actions — be it through mindful eating, restorative sleep, or expressive movement — you satisfy your needs and digest these moments by integrating their benefits into your being. This is not just about the absence of hunger or the ability to move, but rather about *how* your movement and the *quality* of your experiences satisfy your specific needs.

Do you have a bounce in your step or a kink in your neck? Tracking how your body feels provides a good indicator of your energy level, balance, and alignment with your body's rhythms and needs. Body-centric satiation allows your vitality to become a new metric of success, while your innate creativity becomes an important resource, allowing you to engage with life's demands with resilience and vigor.

In the heart center, satiation is expressed as moments of intimacy that address our need for connection, belonging, and participation. Recognizing and appreciating these moments involves more than just surface interactions; it is about delving into the depth of your relationships, feeling the mutual exchange of support, empathy, and love that these relationships create. This process is all about finding the satisfiers that work for you.

As you discover the strength and courage to do so, you allow moments of authentic connection to shape your capacity for compassion and understanding. By deepening these bonds, you allow them to compound into a network of shared experiences and affections, laying the foundation of emotional wealth built on the investment of connection with both others and ourselves. In the heart, satiation fosters a deep knowing that you belong. Stepping into belonging requires that you learn who you are as you practice the art of giving and receiving. Digesting these moments occurs when you appreciate these connections for the impactful experiences that they are and when you embrace vulnerability by opening your heart. And with that profound sense of belonging comes a natural motivation to fully participate in your overlapping communities, which then becomes your normal way of being in the world.

In the mind, satiation reveals itself as moments of growth. As you allow yourself to be fulfilled by these experiences, you naturally satisfy your need for understanding, purpose, and freedom. These moments are born out of the sparks of insight, ongoing learning, and clarity that expand your understanding of the world and your place in it.

To truly appreciate these moments, you must both acquire and integrate knowledge, allowing it to reshape your perspectives and inform your decisions. It is akin to the growth mindset view, where talent and intelligence can grow with practice and effort. Digesting meaning in our mind turns information into wisdom and allows you to cultivate an inner richness that defines success not by the mere acquisition of facts but by the ability to expand personal horizons. This, in turn, brings about a sense of purpose and freedom. In this way, every lesson learned and every idea explored contribute to your composite of intellectual satisfaction, highlighting your mind's journey as an integral part of embodied wealth.

The journey toward satiation is a multifaceted pursuit, interweaving the physical, social, intellectual, and spiritual dimensions of our lives. By recognizing and appreciating experiences of abundance, vitality, growth, and intimacy, we find meaning. We enrich our experience of being in the world, allowing each facet to nourish and guide us toward a deeply rooted sense of fulfillment.

Each of these acts of satiation in our different centers is an economic activity. They encompass moments where there is an input of resources to produce a specific "service or good," either for yourself or for others. This simple exchange is what makes it an economic activity. They don't necessarily need to produce a profit; instead, their purpose is to create embodied wealth.

Satiation Differs from Gratitude

While both are important, satiation and gratitude are distinct feelings. Satiation is a state of fulfillment that arises when our needs — physical, emotional, intellectual, and spiritual — are fully met. It's a deep sense of contentment that comes from within. On the other hand, gratitude is an emotive response, a conscious acknowledgment of the goodness in our lives. Appreciating the positive effects that both things and people have on our daily existence stirs the heart and fosters a sense of connection and belonging.

Gratitude can be a potent antidote to feelings of scarcity, promoting a shift in focus from what is lacking to the abundance that exists in our lives. Consider the transformative experience that occurs when you reflect on what you're thankful for. The sheer act of feeling this gratitude helps shift our perspective from negativity to positivity. It is a powerful catalyst that helps you see the metaphorical glass as half full.

The common phrase "I don't want to seem ungrateful, but…" is a great example of how satiation and gratitude differ. We usually follow this phrase by an admission that something did not quite work out. We can feel thankful for something that someone has done for us or that we have received, but that does not always lead to satisfaction. In fact, sometimes our gratitude provokes negative reactions such as frustration and annoyance, and may inadvertently draw our attention to what is missing. For example, receiving an inheritance can come with the loss of a loved one. We are grateful and grieving simultaneously. Or we can sell a house at a financial gain and mourn the loss of community, land, and memories. Alongside gratitude, we can feel lots of additional emotions, hence fulfillment can't be guaranteed. Satiation is the experience of feeling met by life, where triumphs and challenges are digested as meaning.

Satiation allows for a more nuanced approach to meeting our human needs. It provides a visceral barometer that helps us track what wealth and satisfaction *feel* like and identify the methods to enhance those experiences in our daily life. Our focus shifts from wealth accumulation to wealth creation, as we recognize that what we are looking to create is an experience of embodied wealth. As the barometer rises, we gain confidence in our voice, find our rightful place, and feel a sense of belonging. In that process, money is not so much the object we strive to acquire and hold on to but instead a means to an end.

> ## • MINI MOMENT •
> What's one thing I have received recently that I am grateful for but not necessarily satisfied by?

Digesting Gratitude to Create Satiation

Now, let's look at the process of digesting gratitude to create satiation. Imagine the presence of a person in your life you are grateful for. They might offer a quality you enjoy, a skill that is useful, or a relationship and connection you can count on.

Picture this person in your mind. We will walk through the

three-step process to embody the wealth that comes through gratitude. This involves recognizing and appreciating the person, digesting your gratitude for them by integrating and releasing whatever is most impactful, and finally satiating by compounding the gratitude you feel by embodying the feelings of meaning they inspire in you.

Let's begin. Take a couple of deep breaths to center yourself and access your full attention. Recognize the specific ways this person has affected your life. It might be one specific thing, or you might find yourself running through an entire list. Allow the process of acknowledgment to unfold naturally and according to its own pace and manner. The most important thing is to feel the full impact of your gratitude for this person.

Next, imagine yourself moving from gratitude to a place of appreciation. This might come in the form of a smile, a hug, a bow, a silent word of appreciation, or the placing of your hand on your heart. Allow yourself to move into whatever form of appreciation feels most natural.

Now, let's move to a more subtle part of the process. Digest whatever nourishment is available to you through this relationship by accessing your feelings of appreciation and gratitude. This may take a little more guidance, so follow along as I describe the process. Adjust the practice so that it aligns with what is most alive for you.

As you recognize and appreciate your gratitude for this person in your life, notice the sensations in your body, the images that arise in your mind, the emotions that bubble up in your heart, and the reactions evoked in your spirit. Perhaps your body feels warm and held, or maybe excited and inspired. There is no right way to feel. The process is uniquely yours.

Close your eyes. Allow the feelings, sensations, images, and inspirations to fill you up, one cell at a time. Be sure to take your time. Notice how what started as basic gratitude is turning into something more than feelings of appreciation in your body. As your body begins to feel full of meaning, perhaps even tingling, you naturally evoke the process of digesting these important moments in your life. Notice how an experience of gratitude begins to transform to include feelings of being supported, guided, and inspired. As our gratitude fills us up, we experience a sense of satiation and embodied wealth. This is the crucial part of the process, so take the time to drink these experiences in.

Digestion often involves two interrelated paths — integration and release. Whatever nourishment serves us gets integrated. The experiences that don't are dissolved. For example, there may be some aspects of the relationship with this person that may feel lackluster or even disappointing. Maybe this person evokes strong feelings of anger, anxiety, or resentment, which can be moved through and released.

This is natural. We are complex people, and interactions with the same person can take on all kinds of meaning. The important thing to keep in mind is not only to focus on the positive but also to allow for a full range of interactions to be present. All experiences can have meaning. As you guide yourself to digest the meaningful moments and integrate their nourishment, you also learn how to digest the more challenging ones. Make sure you do both.

This is important. We already made the point that pushing money away takes as much effort as holding it close. The same principle applies here. Recognizing the harder edges in your relationship helps you digest them, instead of unconsciously keeping them at bay. The challenges, missed communications, and even the conflicting feelings of gratitude, frustration, disgust, or jealousy toward the same person all have value. You don't need to preserve the fear or anxiety you feel around this person, but you do need to digest it. This can be a little harder, but take the time to feel the rough edges of these experiences. By identifying and acknowledging them, you can digest and release them from your life. This might look like taking a deep exhale. Or touching the ground and allowing what you don't want to physically flow out of you. You might let go by writing a letter, even if it's never sent. You might speak to a trusted friend or professional. Go ahead and experiment. Finding your own way to digest challenges is essential for genuine self-care.

After you integrate or release these experiences, move to the final step — compounding meaning. Widen your awareness to include other moments in your life that evoke the same feelings of appreciation you have for this person. If you cannot think of anything, hold the intention to recall similar moments in the future. The goal is to compound meaning so that we feel satiated, creating the power of enough in our lives.

As you ground into your feelings of satiation, both with what you choose to keep and what you decide to let go of, you begin to know you are enough. You have agency to design your life, compounding what is working and carving out what is not. Take time to be with the aftermath of this meditation.

> ● MINI MOMENT ●
>
> What did I integrate that I can connect to other moments of meaning in my life?

When we embody these experiences of satiation, the gratitude we started with permeates our entire being. By taking the time to recognize and appreciate, digest through integration and/or release, and finally compound meaning in such a way that we feel satiation, we have allowed ourselves a precious realization — that through those moments of gratitude, we can know in our bones that we are enough and have enough.

As we follow the steps above, we can digest the meaning that is available through our impactful experiences. As we shift our focus from accumulating more stuff to compounding more meaning, we can integrate the meaning that our inheritance brings while also digesting the feelings of loss. By grounding wealth in our bodies, we feel more in touch with ourselves and the material world. Our focus shifts from wealth accumulation to wealth creation as we recognize that what we are looking to create is an experience of embodied wealth in our lives.

When we are satiated, money is less of an object we strive to acquire and hold on to and more of a guide, a technology, and a tool that can help us open new doors and explore new possibilities. Wealth is not a possession, but rather an experience to be had. As we follow these steps toward embodied wealth, the sense of satiation we feel gives us permission to experience wealth without having to control it. And as we proceed down this path, we find we are more equipped to confront our fears of losing our material resources. This allows us to develop and practice feelings of trust, with both money and the world.

A dear friend of mine who is a coach asks her clients at the end of every session, "What is the next small step that you're willing to take?" This question reminds us that we can focus on identifying the next thing to lead us toward a more meaningful and authentic life. We can put that next step into practice and embody the meaning it offers us through the process we have been using here. We can gauge the meaning that has been brought into our life on our scale of satiation, which enables us to lay the foundation for embodying wealth one block at a time.

Satiation takes us beyond the goal of accumulating more money, toward a life where the primary focus is recognizing and discovering the unique ways we can fulfill our needs. Learning about our needs expands our notion of wealth. By experimenting with methods to satisfy our needs, we gain invaluable insights into how to engage with the material world in a way that fosters generosity, fulfillment, and satisfaction, rather than promoting hoarding, unconscious consumption, and waste.

> ### • MINI MOMENT •
>
> What is the next small step toward satiation I am willing to take?

Saturation, Boundaries, and the Limits of Enough

One of the principles in taking care of ourselves requires setting boundaries and making difficult decisions that align with our values. This involves recognizing our limits, saying no when necessary, and not allowing ourselves to be overburdened by societal pressures or professional demands. Real self-care is about setting boundaries regularly, which in turn can lead to empowerment and positive changes in various aspects of life.

In my practice, I help people get clear on what they need less of. Less can lead to more. For example, we revisit categories in their cash flow that may expose unconscious spending (which we gently refer to as money leaks). Or we access jobs and commitments that no longer feel useful or investments that feel out of alignment with their values. In most cases, we intuitively know something needs to shift, but we need some guidance and support in designing the best way to accomplish this goal.

One of my clients, Daniel, had overextended his time working for a prominent Bay Area tech company. He was resentful and tired but could not commit to leaving. He and his wife had participated in a company liquidity event, which yielded a substantial amount of cash to work with. We designed a clear plan of financial independence, including strategies of diversification, tax planning, and creating streams of passive income. Despite our work, he couldn't seem to resign.

We spent months crafting this transition plan. As we dug deeper, we discovered things that still needed to be digested. First, Daniel wanted to ensure his team would be in a good place after his departure. Second, he held on to strong emotional ties to his work. Third, there was a genuine concern that he would be unable to find the same level of creative collaboration, interaction, and community outside of work. And lastly, he felt shackled by golden handcuffs — if he quit, he would forfeit the additional vesting of his stock.

Over time, he recognized that more than money, he required time and space (leisure and curiosity) to explore new strategies that would uncover a deeper sense of purpose. We set a target date, and every time a desire to push the date out arose, we asked, "Is it worth it?" and "Does it add or detract from my sense of enough?" and opened spaces for quiet listening to access what wanted to emerge.

Daniel also remembered that his father had modeled for him a natural sense of contentment. Once that connection was made, digested, and compounded in his awareness, he found the resolution to stick to the plan and transition into the next chapter of his life. He wanted to find that sense of satisfaction for himself.

According to acclaimed novelist Haruki Murakami, "Pain is inevitable, but suffering is optional." Pain and emotional tenderness are a natural part of life, but holding on to things beyond their expiration date can cause undue suffering. Practices of satiation and embracing the power of enough create containers that help us better recognize, establish, and celebrate boundaries, which is a key aspect of crafting and designing the life you want.

In the past, I, too, found that one of the hardest things to do is to say no. Requests that I couldn't meet would feel extremely stressful. I would get a wave of emotion that started out as anxiety but quickly turned to aggravation that someone was asking something of me. Yet I couldn't find the right way to set the boundary, much less feel nourished by this situation. I shied away from saying no, and my lack of limits created an energetic leak that wasted my emotional resources.

It has taken years of self-reflection, personal awareness, and therapy to understand that I am not responsible for meeting everybody's needs. I also had to implement processes that allowed my team to decline an engagement on my behalf and redirect a client to someone who was excited and more readily available to meet their request. I have learned to take in my no as an act of kindness and satiation. Setting a boundary and saying no makes space for someone else to step in and say yes. In fact, I was able to see that saying no fostered an important belief of mine — that there is enough to go around. By knowing my limits and standing by them, I fomented a shared economy that offers many ways to meet a person's needs.

Satiation is that place of just enough — that place where our desires have been met, and we no longer feel a sense of lack or scarcity. Too little leaves us craving more and potentially using the wrong strategies to satisfy our needs. We mistake consumption for real nourishment, leaving us resembling hungry ghosts. Overconsumption leads to overload. When we are overcommitted, we feel the scarcity of time. When we are overloaded with responsibilities at work, we feel burned out. When we have more than enough money, we can get lost trying to figure out what to do with it. Yet even that can feel empty if we feel disconnected from an inherent purpose or cause.

• MINI MOMENT •

What is one thing I need to set a boundary with or say no to now in my life?

The Power of Enough

Satiation is that *just right* feeling that is unique to us in a particular moment. Because it is so specific to that situation, we need to put practices in place to help us remember why we were fulfilled at that time. We might overspend at first as we try new things, or we might hoard our resources until we learn to trust that conscious spending can help address experiences of lack. In both cases, we need to practice graciousness with ourselves and others. And we need to write this down. Learning how to compound meaning so that we feel satiation is not a linear process. It takes time to practice being with ourselves in this way. And we will make mistakes. But if we are clear on the direction and the goal of embodying wealth instead of possessing it, we radically transform the possibility of experiencing wealth almost every step of the way. Before we get to the practice, I would like to share the experience one of my client's had keeping her own satiation journal.

Madelena had a habit of overextending herself, sacrificing her own needs while giving away her precious time and energy to meet the needs of others. This was a clear depiction of the martyr archetype, a pattern by which someone uses sacrifice and suffering to hide the places where they struggle, which limits their ability to address their own needs.

Through some guided meditations, we asked Madelena's martyr to take a break on an imaginary hammock, inviting her to drop her guard and tell us what really was going on. Once relaxed, this part of herself shared that when she sacrificed her time and needs for others, she felt important and valuable. It loved that Madelena had chosen to pursue a career as a therapist. She could help people navigate their needs and get paid for it.

But as she softened the energy produced by this habit of taking care of everyone else, a new story emerged. Madelena began to feel hollow inside. She realized that her actions were blocking her own ability to genuinely show up. Her desire to sacrifice was also producing unchecked anger and resentment, and as a result, she inadvertently pushed people away. This became a wake-up call for Madelena — she needed to learn a new way of relating to people, both personally and professionally, in order to stop blocking parts of herself.

After keeping her satiation journal for a month, Madelena reported:

> This satiation practice has become the place where I notice moments of pleasure and delight in service of letting the goodness of life in, of savoring it. I come to the page to capture the moments when I zoom in and let the feeling of satiation saturate my perspective. Most of the time it is in the quiet, mundane moments: the blue morning light and quiet as I wake up, the way the leaves shimmer in the springtime breeze, the feeling of making a meal with the fresh ingredients I gathered, reading a good book on the couch, the satisfaction of a connective moment with someone I love, or even a stranger. This satiation practice has changed the way I experience the world around me. Where there was once a focus on *What's missing?* there is now the quiet, steady, still attention on what feels whole and imperfect and real: *What simple moment offered itself to me to be felt fully?*

Over time, Madelena was able to heal the parts of herself that felt empty and lacking. By filling her cup with moments of meaning, she compounded the meaning in her life and felt lasting satiation. She drank before she poured. Madelena was moving toward a new kind of wealth that allowed her to relax her critical eye while building what she thought of as "agency," an ability to appreciate the actions she took in the world. She learned that her feeling of disconnection wasn't caused by money but rather by having never been taught to feel satiation. As she worked the practices of embodying wealth, she felt empowered to carve out time for leisure and creativity, which was what she truly craved.

PRACTICE: Keeping a Satiation Journal

The practice of satiation is extremely simple. It requires finding a moment in your day to pause and reflect on one thing that satiated you and then writing it down. You might even choose to have a dedicated journal to keep track of your insights. The intention is to capture the ways you experience feeling satisfied in your life.

My satiation practice happens in the morning. Each day when I wake up, instead of reaching for my phone, I reach for my satiation journal. I close my eyes and relive the events of the previous day. I ask myself what satiated me, and I write it down. Some days, I'll have a list of three or four items. Other days, it is only one. There is hardly ever a day when I can't think of anything.

Step 1: Commit to the Practice

Choose a period you can commit to, such as first thing in the morning or last thing at night. Or bookend your day with a satiation entry. I invite you to practice this exercise for at least a month.

Step 2: Write Out a Daily Entry

Every day, at your allotted time, take three to five minutes to jot down a response to the following question: What satiated me today? Or in Madelena's words, "What simple moment offered itself to me to be felt fully?" If you feel stuck, you can also ask, What can I release to feel more satisfaction in my life?

When you begin, give yourself permission to freely express what comes out. Treat this as an open inquiry to gather data about what works and what doesn't. You can even write out the things that did not satiate or may have created a negative return on your time investment. All of it is valuable.

Step 3: Digest the Commonalities

After the committed time passes (e.g., thirty days), reread all your entries. Pay attention to the commonalities. Is there a particular activity or situation that shows up often? Are there frequent threads that overlap? As we become more aware of feeling satiated, we learn what strategies encourage and nourish embodied satisfaction, and we naturally gravitate toward them and reduce what feels empty and void.

Picking up my satiation journal first thing in the morning, instead of reaching for my phone, helps me start my day in a different energetic space. I feel more connected to myself, versus seeking recognition from others, and I am reminded to bring awareness to my needs as I go about my day. Am I working on creativity? Or on my sense of belonging, understanding, or identity? Do I need to address safety and protection? Or connection?

When I am clear on what I am working on, I can shape my day to make sure I choose the strategies and activities that serve me best, even if it means changing my plans. Or if I can't, at least I'm aware of why I'm choosing not to address that need and mapping out when I will get to it. In the end, I am learning about the true satisfiers that satiate me, because my everyday experience is telling me what is fulfilling and what is not.

Chapter 8 Takeaways

Redefining Success through Satiation: This chapter encourages a paradigm shift from conventional success metrics to a holistic understanding characterized by satiation, highlighting the transformative impact of fully digesting and integrating one's experiences.

Embodying Wealth beyond Materialism: It emphasizes the concept of embodied wealth, where success is measured by the quality and depth of experiences, rather than the accumulation of material possessions, advocating for a balanced approach to consumption that nurtures personal and communal well-being.

Cultivating a Practice of Satiation: The narrative illustrates the importance of developing a consistent practice of recognizing, appreciating, and integrating meaningful moments, showcasing how this practice leads to a sustainable sense of contentment and a profound realization of having enough.

PART 3

Tools for
EMBODYING
Wealth

Chapter Nine

WRITING YOUR MONEY STORY

Turning Taboos into Treasure

Your stories hold power. They play a crucial role in your life, shaping your perceptions, behaviors, and relationships. From the childhood stories you grew up with to the cultural myths that go unnoticed in your life, your narratives help you make sense of the world and your place within it. This is particularly true when it comes to your stories about money, which have a profound impact on your financial well-being and the lives of those you love.

It's no secret that our current narratives about money are often rooted in ideas of scarcity and lack. In some extreme cases, we tie it to evil and greed, driving us to accumulate resources to fill a perceived void. These stories, motivated by desires that stem from a sense of something missing, can lead to unhealthy financial behaviors and a distorted view of wealth. To transform your life, you must create new money stories and shift your mindset from one of scarcity to one of satiation and abundance. And it will take time. This process is not as easy as telling a new story and watching our lives change for the better. We must work at transmuting the old stories that are hidden deep in our bones.

The practice of this chapter will help you rewrite your stories about money into more uplifting narratives and provide a tool you can consistently revisit. By now, you have already learned much about your relationship with money and the importance of turning toward it as an important guide in your life. Now, it is time to get creative and put your insights into story form. I encourage you to write new money stories that align with your values and a broader definition of wealth — one that encompasses meaningful experiences and personal growth. By engaging with your narrative around wealth, you can tap into your own unique experience of the power of enough.

A word of caution — this is not a practice that can be done once and considered done. Stories have lives of their own. They intersect with one another in complex, nonlinear ways. Yet diving deep into your money story can uncover treasures buried within the taboos, akin to finding golden nuggets of insight deep in your financial soil.

I have not encountered a single person who has told me their financial journey unfolded precisely as they thought it would. I've gained a profound appreciation for how important it is to appreciate the twists and turns that are a natural part of every individual's life. In this chapter, I ask you to write stories about money that embrace all the challenges, setbacks, and failures you have experienced. It is important to see these as opportunities for learning and growth. And don't forget to celebrate your successes as well. I want you to commit to seeing your life as meaningful, no matter how hard it's been. I encourage you to connect the dots between satiation and fulfillment.

These narratives illuminate the disparities between your initial life expectations and your current reality. They also help illustrate how all those twists and turns, the highs and lows in your journey, have been instrumental in shaping the amazing person you have become. Courageously sharing your stories and confronting the unforeseen both unveils your humanity and uncovers the clarity and consciousness born from navigating the tumultuous ride.

Sharing Money Stories: You Can't Seem to Win

We love sharing tips on how to make money, but when it comes to revealing our personal experiences with money, a normal conversation can become awkward and quickly grind to a halt. If telling our stories about money is so important, why is it that talking about money is still one of our biggest cultural taboos?

Money often presents us with a peculiar catch-22, a paradoxical situation in which we face challenges and suffer whether we have an abundance of money or a lack of it. This conundrum can leave us feeling trapped and frustrated, as we struggle to find a balanced and fulfilling relationship with our finances.

On the one hand, not having enough money may lead to negative emotions and practical difficulties. Financial scarcity can engender stress, anxiety, and a sense of powerlessness. We might also feel a real hunger as we fight to provide for ourselves and our loved ones. Lack of resources can also limit our opportunities and choices, making it harder to pursue our goals and dreams.

On the other hand, having an abundance of money can present its own set of challenges. Wealth can complicate relationships, leading to feelings of guilt, shame, isolation, or resentment. It can also create a sense of pressure and responsibility, as we grapple with the expectations and demands that come with financial success. It can be a lot to manage.

A large influx of money can be both euphoric and overwhelming, leading to hasty decisions. Some people will give large sums away. Others will succumb to family members asking for support. Some will invest in large purchases (like homes), unaware of the ongoing financial commitment it takes to sustain them. In the extreme case of winning a lottery or receiving a windfall, a sudden flood of money can ironically hinder our ability to discover how to generate it for ourselves. This can inadvertently impede the development of healthy financial skills. And because we don't know how and where to talk about money, our personal experiences are often riddled with confusion and shame.

When we don't have safe spaces to talk about money, we stay trapped in vicious cycles, repeating money stories that are harmful to everyone, including ourselves. We yearn to work through our confusing thoughts and emotions about money. We have so many questions to ask, but we don't have the people, places, and tools to do so. It is like needing experience to get a job, yet needing a job to get experience.

By recognizing that both scarcity and abundance can present challenges, we can begin to develop a more nuanced and balanced approach to money. This involves focusing on fulfilling a greater spectrum of human needs to create genuine success, rather than solely pursuing financial gain.

My clients consistently struggle with this balancing act. Some come in the door wanting help redistributing their wealth. They are ashamed of having too much money and need help with how to give it away. In fact, some even try to donate anonymously because they don't want to be judged for having so much to begin with. I also have clients who feel ashamed that they have so little money. They want support in understanding how the financial system works and how to best utilize it, and yet are ashamed to admit they don't have a lot to work with. It feels like no matter how little or how much money we have, we can't win.

Ultimately, navigating this catch-22 requires a willingness to embrace the complexity and paradoxes of our relationship with wealth. By rewriting our money stories to emphasize meaning, balance, and personal growth, we can develop a more resilient and fulfilling approach to financial well-being. This involves recognizing that money is just one piece of the larger puzzle of a rich and satisfying life.

Bringing Stories to Light

Before we begin rewriting our own stories, it will be helpful to get a better sense of why these stories have so much power over us. Storytelling has evolved as a tool for survival, shaping how societies value and interact with money. In his book *The Storytelling Animal*, Jonathan Gottschall explores how stories have been essential to human development and how we engage with one another. He makes a case that our ability to create and share myths and stories is precisely what has allowed us to navigate complex social situations, pass on knowledge, and cultivate a sense of shared identity.

Yuval Noah Harari writes at length about the important role that myths and stories have played throughout our human evolution. In his book *Sapiens: A Brief History of Humankind*, he shares that "money isn't a material reality — it is a psychological construct," and that "money is the most universal and most efficient system of mutual trust ever devised." In other words, and as discussed in chapter 2, stories like those we tell about money are a social technology for the exchange of trust and value. The art of sharing these stories fosters our ability to trust relative strangers and enables large-scale human cooperation.

Financial realities are created through the power of shared myth, and specifically our stories about money. When we look closely, this point becomes a lot more personal. This chapter is all about your individual story with money. Chapter 10 will bring it back to the context of shared stories, our financial DNA, and the greater collective.

Recent research in the neuroeconomics of trust has revealed how sharing our stories can influence not only our economic behavior but also our sense of self. It highlights how compelling narratives can trigger the release of oxytocin, leading to increased empathy, connection, and cooperation. The more powerful the emotional engagement, the higher the release of oxytocin. By understanding the psychological and neurological underpinnings of our money stories, we can recognize the power that they hold over our financial decisions and behaviors.

Less compelling stories produce the opposite effect. When we have unprocessed emotions around money such as fear, shame, and confusion, we tend to hold our money stories close. When we do this, we deprive ourselves of the healing qualities that storytelling brings. We become reserved and judge those who speak about money freely, secretly jealous of their capacity to do so. We may categorize them as ostentatious and pretentious. We've all done it before.

But here's the catch — stories are transformed by bringing them to light. When we find safe spaces and people who can acknowledge the complexity of life with us, the act of bringing awareness to these stories can lessen their hold.

Stories as a Storehouse of Power

Your stories about money are a storehouse of power. Within your stories lie both the source of your being and the power of your purpose. What if instead of feeling ashamed, guilty, or hesitant when talking about money, you embraced your money stories and saw in them an infinite supply of insight, potentiality, and strength? Sounds amazing, right?

If we saw money in this way, we would start swapping money stories all day long! We'd be happy to learn from our own and other people's mistakes. We would satisfy our need for learning and understanding and find new avenues for freedom, connection, and participation. In other words, we would discover new satisfiers and new strategies for living a life of embodied wealth, hidden within these nuggets of gold.

By focusing on the narratives we create around money, we can align our financial behaviors with our values and aspirations. This shift in perspective requires us to view money as a social technology that helps us harness the power of story to shape our lives.

Changing our stories about money from ones of scarcity and accumulation to those of inspiration and fulfillment can alter both personal and collective economic behaviors. When we view wealth as the abundance of meaningful experiences, we are more likely to make financial decisions that prioritize personal growth, relationships, and community well-being.

Emotions as a Form of Currency and Wealth

As you bring self-awareness to the ways that you tell your stories, you increase your emotional intelligence. And as you become fluent in the language of emotions, you find that it is easier both to be with your own feelings and to empathize with the emotions of those around you. At the end of the day, emotions are energy in motion. They are a form of currency.

Being stuck in old stories and hard memories makes us feel poor and confused. When our stories about money remain unprocessed, they hijack our life energy. We all know what it feels like to churn in anger, worry incessantly, or drown in grief. It's amazing how we have these precise metaphors to describe how we get bogged down by emotions, as being stuck in our feelings is very real.

When you keep your money stories private, not only do you miss the opportunity to commune with others, but you are also depriving yourself. Keeping your stories inside is like hoarding; it becomes hard to open and share. Yet, we have a preconceived notion that if we keep our stories confined, we hold our vulnerability at bay and remain safe.

The problem with hoarding your money stories is that it comes at a big expense. Remember the exercise in chapter 4 about holding on to money too tightly? Hoarding our stories is similar. It requires effort, and excessive privacy can cause anger, resentment, and depression. We feel resentful because no one understands our situation, but we fail to recognize that we haven't revealed enough of ourselves for that understanding to occur.

When we stockpile our money stories instead of exchanging them, they risk becoming stagnant, undigested, and even burdensome. In some cases, unprocessed stories can become poisonous and lead to disease. Regardless of where we fall on the spectrum of financial wealth, one thing is true: we each have a money story to tell, and our capacity to share and digest it affects our overall money health. Sharing our story allows our relationship with money to find its *appropriate* place.

Our stories about money help us make sense of our wealth mandala. They shed light, bring nuance, and emphasize the connective threads of new strategies we can employ as we build holistic wealth. Our different memories are the inventory that show us which strategies worked and which ones didn't. We can release the tactics that have expired and strengthen the ones that add to our experience of wealth. By turning toward our stories, we awaken creativity and new possibilities. We find the courage to break personal and familiar patterns, and we build inspiration and support to try something new.

Experiencing choice and the ability to exert influence in your life can make you feel powerful. To design your life from a place of power requires that you turn to your past and release the gems hidden in your memories. It also requires you to keep an eye on the future and a commitment to planning. When you look backward and liberate your personal capital, you may even be inspired to design your wealth plan in new and unique ways.

The first time I wrote out my money story, I was shocked to realize how many good memories I had with money. I recall getting an allowance at age twelve and riding my bike with my friends to the nearest drugstore to buy whatever candy I wanted. I had freedom of choice, within the boundaries of whatever my allowance could buy.

I remember being a Girl Scout and walking the halls of the hospital where my dad worked. He'd take an hour off from seeing patients to go knocking on the other physicians' doors with me as I sold my Girl Scout cookies. My dad's enjoyment in connecting with his colleagues taught me the confidence to make a sale, collect payment, and deliver a product.

I can also see my mom sitting at her desk, balancing our checkbook. She was the bill payer in the family. She taught me how to keep clear books and ledgers, which I still practice to this day.

The harder memories with money came later in life. My parents taught me financial organization and the importance of saving, but they did not teach me how to invest. I was taught the importance of good credit, and yet in my twenties I still went into debt. I was encouraged to follow my passions, but it took me over a decade to figure out how to craft an entrepreneurial career that sustained me. I know what it feels like to walk into a bank and be told that you're not qualified for a loan, and what it feels like to live paycheck to paycheck with no savings to fall back on.

Over time, I have learned to work with money to create a strong wealth foundation. As with any relationship, my emotions with money go up and down, but my overall dynamic with it is healthy and vibrant. I trust I have enough. I have built confidence in my ability to earn. And I have learned how to save, invest, and spend in ways that best support my wide array of needs.

After working with clients for decades, I know that not everyone has been so lucky. Money stories are filled with instances of hardship, suffering, and adversity. Material lack is real. Premature deaths of parents, which can significantly alter a family's financial foundation, occur more frequently than we would like to acknowledge. Stock markets crash. We make bad investments. We lose houses and other material possessions in natural disasters. War forces us out of our countries and communities. Financial disparity opens doors of opportunity and access for some people but not for others.

All these experiences shape us and can even define us. As conscious humans, we have the capacity to rise from the ashes and design a different future by cultivating the strength and courage needed to heal from our past.

Transforming Your Money Story

In her groundbreaking work on how women lead creative and fulfilling lives, Mary Catherine Bateson uses the metaphor of "composing a life." She offers a framework for rewriting our personal narratives and encourages us to view our stories as malleable, capable of being reshaped to align with our values, aspirations, and perspectives on ourselves. We are the authors of our own lives, and through conscious composition of our narratives, we can create more meaningful and fulfilling existences. Her work invites us "to look at problems in terms of the creative opportunities they present."

Narrative integration allows us to reconcile conflicting beliefs and experiences, thus offering a more nuanced and adaptive relationship with money. By embracing the complexity of our money stories and actively composing a new narrative, we can develop a more resilient and flexible approach to true wealth creation. The practice below follows in this tradition. I will encourage you to take stock of your personal stories as a way to inventory your own life. Pay close attention to those that seem most challenging to share. Often it is here that taboos are transformed into treasure.

PRACTICE: Transforming Your Money Story

Think back to all your experiences with money and the cultural and/or inherited narratives that have shaped you. All these stories may feel complex or overwhelming at first. In fact, taking this first step into our stories might feel downright daunting. Or it might feel exciting to be starting your journey toward deeper insight and intimacy with the stories that made you. Either way, don't worry, you are not alone. Over the years, I have seen clients have a wide diversity of responses to this practice. And yet, in every individual case, the results have been overwhelmingly positive by the end.

This practice is inspired by Deborah Price, founder of the Money Coaching Institute. She teaches students in her workshops about the power of creating a money biography. The practice below is my own adaptation of her exercise. Make a ritual out of writing your money story. So, get comfy, light some candles, and play some music in the background to help set the mood. You can find a PDF version of the money story grid on my website, ElizabethHusserl.com/resources, if you prefer to download and print it.

Step 1: Write Your Money Memories

Using the money story grid below, start with the first interaction you had with money. Identify how old you were. What was important to you then? Who was with you? What was it like to engage with money? How did you feel about the experience?

Continue to write your money story chronologically. The money story grid is a simple format for recording the main money memories that come to mind from early childhood until today. Adding notes in the margin next to your age can serve as a helpful prompt for recalling stories or experiences from your life.

For example, you can make a note of when you were in elementary, middle, or high school. You can write down the houses you lived in, places you traveled to, or such decisive moments as marriages, births, new jobs, and divorces. Use the age margin to connect to these life events, and then use those moments to ask yourself what your experience with money was at that time. You can also use the age margin to write out the years and connect your money biography with larger local, national, or world events.

Consider adding significant memories that you remember, regardless of whether they directly involved you or not. This may include memories related to your parents, grandparents, and other family members. If there is a time frame during which you cannot recall any memories, leave the space blank for thoughts that may arise later.

You may or may not have many specific money memories. You might write the memories in random order, which will stimulate more memories to come. At some point, memories may start to flood. Write down quick descriptions in the years they pertain to, and then tackle them one at a time.

In the first stage of the exercise, it is not necessary to go into detail about each memory. Rather, just state the memory, your age at the time, and any emotions you recall feeling around the experience.

Money Memories	
My first memory with money	
Ages 0–5	
Ages 6–10	
Ages 11–15	
Ages 16–20	
Ages 21–25	

Ages 26–30	
Ages 31–35	
Ages 36–40	
Ages 41–45	
Ages 46–50	
Ages 51–55	
Ages 56–60	
Ages 61–65	
Ages 66–70	
Ages 71–80	
Ages 81–90	

Step 2: Acknowledge Your Experience

After taking an initial stab at writing out your money stories, put your pen down or close the computer. Notice the predominant emotion, sensation, or thought that stays with you as you finish this first draft. What do you discover? Is this emotion new or old? Is it a recurring thought that you have had about money or a new insight? Is there a sinking sensation somewhere in your body or a tingling aliveness?

Take time to savor what emerged. Remember that to embody wealth, we need to digest and integrate the meaningful moments in our lives. Even the most bitter or sour experience can turn into satiation and satisfaction when we learn how to own what is ours.

Whatever it is, first practice the art of gently embracing and welcoming it. Close your eyes and acknowledge whatever arose. Maybe you choose to speak it out loud, or to touch the part of your body where it is held. Gift yourself the conscious recognition of whatever emerged.

Step 3: Be Your Own Anthropologist

Anthropology is the study of people throughout the world — how they behave, how they adapt to environments, and how they communicate and socialize with one another. Cultural anthropologist Mary Catherine Bateson learned about the lives of women by paying close attention to the ways that she and the people around her lived their lives. This is an opportunity for you to conduct your own ethnographic research.

Read through your money story as if you were an anthropologist. The lens of an anthropologist allows you to take a step back and study your money story more objectively, enabling you to examine your financial history from a new perspective. In fact, autoethnography is a form of research where we use self-reflection to explore anecdotal and personal experiences.

As you review your money story, highlight or mark the phrases that jump out at you. Contemplate the following questions:

- What patterns do you see?

- What catches your attention?

- What words or phrases feel most charged or most aligned?

- What triggers pain?

- What memories resemble one another?

- What patterns start to emerge?

- What connections do you make?

- Who in your past played a strong role in your money biography?

- What role did they play?

- How did their presence in your life make or break your own healthy relationship with money?

Be generous with your insights. You can capture your observations by writing them in a journal, drawing them in a sketchbook, or making a collage that visually represents the significant moments in your chronology. The aim here is to gather the most important takeaways you can glean from your money story. Maybe you discover that you have been an entrepreneur with money all along. I see this often with clients who, from a young age, had lemonade stands, babysitting businesses, or marketed their skills as car washers or dog walkers.

Maybe you realize there was one moment that represented a huge trauma or break in your relationship with money. Good to know. With knowledge comes power. If you can track the break, you can begin the process of restoration and repair.

Maybe you discover the source of your feelings of guilt, embarrassment, or being overwhelmed. Did your parents compare your situation with that of others? If so, was it because you had more or less? If you can remember phrases you heard as a little kid, write them down. Do they still hold power in your life? Are they true?

Step 4: Connect Your Money Story to Your Wealth Mandala

Your money story holds a wealth of information. Memories shed light on your current purpose and power. Taking the time to reflect on your experiences with money can reveal new possibilities for growth or fresh insights on patterns you want to shift. More importantly, your money story can illuminate your wealth mandala and the needs that most require your attention.

Once you have read through your money story in its entirety, go back to the wealth mandala you colored in. Look at the different needs that you recognized as strongest or most fulfilled, and those that felt deficient.

Grab a few index cards or sticky notes. Write down the needs that you feel less satisfied with, or bring them to your conscious awareness. Then go back to your money story. What memories connect to these needs? How have your life experiences supported your needs? And in what ways have you faced events that potentially shut down the fulfillment of a need or even violated it?

Next, write the names of the needs that you currently feel satisfied with in the margin next to the memories they are connected to. Then, take a step back. See what information you can gather on how you have successfully addressed your needs in the past, as well as the ways you kept the satisfaction of these at bay. What new strategies or possibilities do you see?

Congratulations! You have completed your first money story. But remember that this is called a practice for a reason. If you want to create lasting change and transformation in your life, you must think of this as an ongoing activity. For example, you can create a ritual where at the end of your week you journal about the most important money experience you had. Or you can share this practice with a friend and schedule times to exchange money stories. Be creative. Perhaps you might even bring in humor. There is no one way to transform your money story, but it starts with the recognition that you have one.

My Path toward Belonging

When I connected my money story to my wealth mandala, it became clear that I have been working on my need for belonging, connection, and purpose from a very early age. I was raised in a world of financial health and privilege. My parents worked hard to create an environment of safety and security. My dad was a doctor, and my mom was a therapist. We lived in a household of plenty. Growing up, I received everything I needed for financial stability, love and safety, and more.

Yet, as in all households, there were gaps that marked me. My mother was so focused on keeping our Colombian heritage alive that she overlooked the importance of teaching me how to connect and belong to the new culture we were part of in Louisiana. In contrast, my dad flourished in his role as a doctor in the United

States and shared this excitement with me. During my childhood, I observed an evident tension between my parents as they deliberated at large between staying in New Orleans or returning to Colombia. I struggled to discover a sense of belonging between these two worlds.

I didn't feel like I fit in with the Southern culture I was raised in. I loved the music and New Orleans's natural inclination to celebrate almost anything, but I still felt like I was out of place. My vibrant Latin identity was celebrated in our extended community gatherings, but it was not as prevalent in my friend circles or at school. My childhood had financial stability, but along with it came emotional strain and an uncertainty around cultural roots. Many times, I felt like an outsider, an intruder, and inferior.

In writing my money story, I noticed that although I had monetary resources at my disposal, I lacked a core sense of belonging in this world. I experienced a close-knit family who deeply loved me, but we were from a different place and culture from most of the people around us. The result was a particular kind of scarcity that affected a distinct set of needs. I had security, safety, love, care, and financial resources in my youth but lacked a sense of deep connection or belonging with friends.

It has taken me decades to find my place. I have traveled the world to experience diverse locations, narratives, and cultures. At times, I have held on to relationships longer than I should or given up core parts of myself, desperately wanting to fit in. I've even felt disdain toward money because it could not buy the true experience I was looking for.

When I turned twenty-six, I wrote out a contract for my life. I had recently returned from my two-year stint in Oaxaca and felt it was clear my life's work wasn't there but in the United States, where people had so much but felt so poor. In my contract, I promised to rediscover my roots and pledged to help people consume less. This was not because I thought consumption was bad per se, but rather because I had an intuitive sense that there was another way. As wisely articulated by one of my mentors, Satish Kumar, when we go to the root of economics and delve within ourselves, we discover that satisfaction rests on our ability to cultivate a healthy sense of self-worth, self-confidence, and purpose in the world. This ability allows us to feel at home in ourselves, ultimately fulfilling our need to know our place in the world and reassuring us that we belong.

It's taken me much time and dedication to figure out that I have a plethora of human needs, and it took even longer to learn how to meet them. Over time, I have not only learned to grow and appreciate my financial resources but also to increase the value of my sense of place in the world. I now feel like I belong.

This is priceless.

Connecting your money story to your wealth mandala can point to what needs may have the biggest impact on your experience of well-being. Gaining this clarity and knowledge is essential to designing a life of embodied wealth.

Chapter 9 Takeaways

Rewrite Your Money Story: Our financial behaviors and sense of wealth are deeply influenced by the stories we tell ourselves about money. To initiate transformative change, we must craft new narratives that foster a mindset of abundance and fulfillment, rather than scarcity and simply filling a void. This requires deep reflection and a commitment to revising our internal scripts about money over time.

Stories Are a Storehouse of Power: Acknowledging that our financial journey is seldom a straight path allows us to appreciate the learning and growth that come from our unique experiences. Instead of perceiving setbacks and challenges as failures, we can view them as valuable lessons that contribute to our comprehensive understanding of wealth.

Money Stories Are a Catalyst for Connection and Transformation: Sharing our personal financial experiences can break cultural taboos and allow us to find community and understanding. By bringing our money stories to the light, we can uncover insights, build empathy, and foster a healthier relationship with wealth that resonates with our true needs and values.

Chapter Ten

UNCONDITIONAL ACCEPTANCE

Asking the Heart to Heal Our Financial DNA

Because we make sense of our experiences of the world through the stories we tell ourselves and others, these narratives shape our identities and guide our actions. In some fundamental way, we are literally the sum of our shared stories. Our myths are more than fairy tales; they are the fabric of our lives. They are very real and kept in our heart, mind, body, and soul. Yet the stories that got us here may not get us there.

In the previous chapter, you explored your personal money story and uncovered insights into your current relationship with money. This chapter delves deeper into the connection between who you are, what you have experienced, and where you come from. Your ancestral narratives and cultural myths play a big role in your financial life. These inherited stories are a vital foundation of your financial identity. You are born into a collective milieu that holds a communal story. It has its own currents, nuances, and colors — much like a canvas that has already been painted with broad strokes and vivid imagery. I have never heard from anyone that their childhood environment or culture played no role in shaping their current relationship with money. In fact, the opposite is true. Yet your financial stories don't have to dictate your life's outcome. You have the agency to design your life, but these stories wield significant influence and power. Think of this as your financial DNA.

To transform your life, it's essential to reexamine your financial DNA by owning and reshaping your stories of scarcity and wealth, without blaming money. Clarifying the connections between your past and present is crucial. As you reshape these narratives, ensure that the strategies and solutions you adopt are relevant and adaptable to your current circumstances. This may seem straightforward, yet it's not always easy. My own personal journey has revealed to me places that were too painful for my grandparents to visit. But as you'll find in your own ancestral stories, it is the hardest knots that, when untangled, produce the biggest release and relief.

Peeling back the layers of your family's financial DNA can be both daunting and enlightening. In your family's history, you may find a number of different stories. Unfortunately, in some cases, the lineage has been fundamentally severed due to slavery, persecution, or war. I am fully aware that evoking an ancestral past might be painful. Unconditional acceptance is a vital tool to help you overcome the trauma caused by severed ties.

For others, there will be times of prosperity worth celebrating alongside periods of adversity that can be equally instructive. These stories of trials and triumphs are critical, as they provide crucial learning opportunities. Understanding how your ancestors responded to challenges, or where they stumbled, offers invaluable lessons in resilience and financial acumen. We can feel exposed when we share our money stories, especially in the cases where you and your loved ones have been challenged and come up short of your goals. Sharing that out loud might provoke a vulnerability hangover, which you fear you may not recover from. It is by sharing these collective stories with people we trust that our relational bonds are tested and formed. The practice of offering unconditional acceptance has been useful and powerful in both my life and my work with clients.

This practice is part of an embodied approach that calls on the wisdom of the body, heart, mind, and soul. Instead of relying on any one of our parts, an embodied approach is integrated and participatory. It asks for the participation both among and within these centers. Our mind has dominated economics and finances for too long, at the expense of the wisdom and richness of our heart, body, and soul. No one center can or should run the show.

> • MINI MOMENT •
>
> What is one money pattern that stems from my financial DNA?
> From whom in my family did I inherit this?

The Power of Unconditional Acceptance

Unconditional acceptance is a simple act of compassion and kindness, one that you can give to yourself right now. It requires that you accept what is and has been for what it is and has been. Acceptance doesn't equal approval; we don't have to like it. Instead, acceptance is the ability to acknowledge the reality of whatever you are living without resistance. In the process, you allow yourself to loosen some of the static energy held in your familial relationship to money.

I want you to take a few deep breaths and connect with your personal experience of the power of enough. Hopefully by now there have been seeds planted and threads woven for you to connect to the truth that you have and are enough. Before we dive into your ancestral lineage, you need to find your core. If you feel stuck, close your eyes and place your hand over your heart. Hear the words *I am enough* gently repeat themselves in your mind space. Take as long as you need repeating this phrase, letting its own rhythm and cadence emerge.

As the repetition of the phrase continues, allow the essence of enough to evoke an energetic experience. See its color, sense its temperature, and feel its texture. Allow it to naturally overflow throughout your body, and as it flows and grows, let every cell of your being drink it in. Feel the depth of meaning within your body, and then gently place your hand on your heart. Repeat these simple words: "I accept you. You are enough. Just as you are." This is how the mind supports the heart — the power of the spoken word. Repeat these words over and over until you feel a sensation in your body that registers that your heart had been heard. This is how the body supports the heart — it communicates when something significant is digested. Let this feeling resonate however and wherever it wants, and then take some time to breathe it in. When you are ready, lower your hand and open your eyes. This is the practice of unconditional acceptance, which is available to you at any point in your day.

There may be a part of you that thinks something so simple cannot have any lasting or meaningful effect. If this voice or any other wants to keep you from this practice, I want you to turn toward that part of yourself, ask it to pause, and invite it to consider how important this is. This practice is not complicated, yet it is profound.

Contemporary research shows that the happiest person on the planet got to be that way by sending loving-kindness to other people. Loving-kindness creates a frequency of brain waves that calms the nervous system and opens the heart. This is the doorway to embodying enough. It is something you can do for yourself every day that will have an outsized impact on the rest of your life. The practice of unconditional acceptance can be applied to yourself and your most vulnerable stories, but it can also be gifted to your family to transform your financial DNA.

Giving love and acceptance may seem straightforward in calm moments, but it becomes more challenging amid the tumult of strong emotions. How, then, can we show up for ourselves and others when it matters most, even when the overwhelming power of our emotions threatens to take over? The key lies in an embodied approach.

This method leverages the synergy among all aspects of our being — body, heart, mind, and soul — to function harmoniously. The heart, on its own, can easily become swamped by emotional intensity. It requires the support of the other centers to manage and channel these emotions effectively. Only then can it offer the gifts of love and acceptance. By engaging all centers, we ensure that our response to emotional challenges is balanced and comprehensive, enabling us to handle moments of high emotional stress with grace and composure.

Wealth Is an Embodied Approach

Unconditional acceptance is not only a profound practice but also a gateway to enhancing emotional intelligence, which is found in the confluence between the mind and the heart. Your level of emotional intelligence — and how effectively you apply it — strongly influences your potential success in various aspects of life, including your relationships and career. Emotional intelligence begins with self-awareness, which involves gaining a clear understanding of and a manageable distance from your emotions. The journey continues through self-regulation, leading to heightened empathy, rekindled motivation, and enhanced social skills.

Self-awareness can begin with a simple realization, such as, Wow, I am experiencing strong emotions right now! This moment of reflexivity, where you recognize and acknowledge your emotional state, is crucial and can manifest in various ways. At its core, self-awareness originates from the mind center, which plays several pivotal roles. It acts as a detached observer that calmly notes what is happening both within and around us. It can also serve as a visionary, imagining future possibilities and pathways. However, the mind has its complexities — it can sometimes become an obsessive and anxious companion, striving to control every aspect of our experience. Understanding these diverse functions of the mind helps us navigate our internal landscapes more effectively, balancing observation and control with vision and creativity.

When our emotions become intense and threaten to overwhelm our heart, the mind steps in to offer the essential spaciousness needed to manage these feelings effectively. The mind's ability to create a certain distance from our emotions is not a matter of disconnection, but rather of providing the clarity needed to process and genuinely experience these feelings. While it might initially seem counterintuitive, considering that we often view the mind as a mechanism for suppressing emotions, its true role is quite beneficial. In moments when emotional intensity could otherwise cloud our judgment or impair our ability to think and react constructively, the mind acts as a moderator. By preventing our emotional responses from becoming overwhelming and causing us to shut down, we can engage with our emotions in a balanced and reflective manner.

Some experts describe the overwhelming experience of strong emotions as our nervous system being "hijacked." This vivid metaphor effectively captures the intensity. When powerful emotions emerge, it can feel as though one is drowning, with survival seemingly dependent on escaping these overwhelming feelings. Often when people exhibit anger or frustration, they aren't truly feeling these emotions deeply; instead, they are experiencing a flood of emotions. This overwhelming surge creates a sense of desperation, prompting them to expel these emotions outward, effectively offloading their intensity onto others in the vicinity. It is precisely at this juncture that the heart must engage and we invite unconditional acceptance into play. But the heart can't do this on its own.

While your heart grapples with emotional turmoil, afraid of being flooded, your mind can rise above the storm. It can step back from the situation and serve as both an observer and a visionary. This approach provides a crucial perspective on the situation, allowing us to approach our emotions with curiosity and an excitement for learning. From this vantage point, the mind is able not only to assess the current emotional landscape but also to envision various paths forward. It can then propose different strategies for responding to the emotional challenge at hand. This dual capability of the mind — to observe and to strategize — provides a stabilizing influence and multiple options on how to proceed.

Like the heart, the mind, too, can become overwhelmed by intense emotional energy, at which point the body must intervene. The body is deeply attuned to the flow of energy and understands how emotional turbulence can infuse our lives with vitality. It naturally seeks to transform the intensity of our emotions into physical motion. When we engage in physical activities, whether it's walking, dancing, stretching, or any form of exercise, the body supports the heart in not getting stuck.

It is the power of this duo — mind and body — that allows your heart the spaciousness and flexibility to feel what's in front of it. And it is in this collaboration that your heart finally finds the spaciousness (provided by the self-awareness of the mind) and time (provided by the self-regulation of the body) to be with what it's feeling. No matter how intense the experience, this embodied approach can lead you to a place where your emotions move through. You'll arrive at a place where you can put your hand on your heart and offer unconditional acceptance to the profound, vibrant, and inherent beauty of the heart realm.

As we gain a working knowledge of our own emotional world, we discover a newfound empathy and understanding for others. This empathy leads to improved social interactions. People feel like we are available and can listen. And as we give ourselves the gift of feeling the depth and breadth of our emotional selves, others will trust us with their emotions too.

Everything you need to transform your relationship with money and wealth is already available. What you need is the natural wisdom of these centers — body, heart, mind — working together through the life of the soul. This embodied approach is less a prescription than an invitation. These words are part of an exercise that encourages you to embrace and appreciate the beautiful dance that is your embodied approach to life. Your body, heart, and mind want to work in tandem for the betterment of your soul.

The transformation you seek is right before you. Your heart, mind, and body want to do things in particular ways that are unique to you and your journey. So I encourage you to find methods to develop your own embodied approach.

• MINI MOMENT •

Think back to the exercise of writing your money story. Choose one thing in that story that you are still struggling to accept.

Now, close your eyes. Place both of your hands on your heart and let the intensity of the emotions arise. All you have to do is feel this intensity for ninety seconds. We can do anything for ninety seconds. If you need one, set a timer on your phone.

Let the waves emerge and overcome you. When the time is up, place one hand on your forehead and one on your belly. Feel the power of your body as it breathes. Allow your breath to become exaggerated, as if you were watching your body retraining your heart's emotions by slowing them down and giving them a rhythmic movement to feel.

Now, bring your awareness to the hand on your forehead. Pause for a moment, then release direct contact and allow your hand to hover in front of your mind's eye. Keep it close enough that you can sense your hand's warmth and presence, but ensure that it does not touch your forehead, thus evoking a degree of spaciousness to foster self-awareness. Don't go too far — the mind can also be overwhelmed, and so you must be careful not to let it run wild. Use this physical reminder of engaged distance to invite your heart to replay the story and its emotions from a slightly de-tached perspective.

What wants to be held and accepted? What does this story, with all its emotions, have to teach you? Feel the answer moving through you like a circuit, starting with the contact of your hand on your belly, moving up your torso into your heart, and streaming outward through your mind. Repeat this cycle as many times as you need. You are a circuit. You can harness your own power. You are enough.

Unconditional Acceptance for Our Financial DNA

As much as our stories are about ourselves, they are also a window into our ancestral past. Yet many of these stories remain hidden. Bringing them into the light of day is often too painful or de-stabilizing. If we resist integrating what feels uncomfortable, the patterns and lessons will continue to affect our lives. There are buried treasures within these stories that hold important keys to transforming our financial DNA.

The closer we look at family patterns that don't go away, the more obvious it becomes that we need to extend the practice of unconditional acceptance to our ancestors. Their stories are our stories. Their narratives shape our identities and guide our actions. It is crucial that we turn toward the past.

Having said that, I need to make something abundantly clear.

I do not believe we are responsible for our ancestors' actions. We are not responsible for their unprocessed stories and emotions. But that does not mean they don't influence how we relate to our wealth and well-being today. This work can be hard, and it requires a delicate dance. There are a lot of difficult things that exist in our pasts. But as challenging as these histories may be, turning away from them won't help anyone. What happened in our familial past influences how we view and interact with the world, and we must confront it so that their actions don't influence our lives in unconscious ways.

In his book *It Didn't Start with You*, Mark Wolynn explores the science of epigenetics, which looks at how our genes can be influenced by our environments and experiences. He argues that trauma can be inherited across generations. The hard truth is that the money traumas experienced by your parents and grandparents can have a direct impact on your beliefs and behaviors. Did someone in your family suffer a substantial financial loss from which they never recovered? Were your ancestors forced from their homeland? Maybe one of your ancestors committed harms against others or themselves, and it feels like this knowledge could overwhelm you with guilt and shame.

Financial DNA is real. If we don't heal these traumas, they will continue to cycle through future generations of our family. It is far too easy to repeat the patterns of our shared past. If you are committed to the growth and transformation required to embody wealth, you will have to practice unconditional acceptance when it comes to the past. I have worked with clients from generations of material wealth who still experience scarcity due to being taught that wealth is only meant to be earned, not enjoyed.

Facing our financial lineage doesn't condemn us to relive family wounds. In fact, it's quite the opposite. The sooner we digest and integrate the challenges of our ancestors, the sooner we stop paying for our past. The process of trauma healing involves using the embodied approach introduced in this chapter to make unconscious experiences conscious. If we can find the spaciousness to be with the emotions that accompany these stories, we might find new ways to move these experiences through our body. This can open the door to feelings of empathy and unconditional acceptance, even for experiences that may seem devastating to acknowledge. The goal is to find a deeper understanding and realize the hidden wealth that is born from this new potential for resolution and peace.

Rachel Yehuda and Mallory E. Bowers are pioneers in epigenetics. Their research shows that the "offspring of severely stress-exposed parents are at risk for adverse outcomes because of enduring epigenetic changes in the parental biological systems." Epigenetics involves changes in gene expression that do not alter the DNA sequence itself but can affect how genes are turned on or off. Severe stress can lead to epigenetic modifications in our ancestral biological systems. We may inherit these epigenetic changes, leading to an increased risk of psychological and physiological issues, which can include heightened vulnerability to stress, anxiety, depression, and other health problems that were initially triggered by our parents' or grandparents' stress.

This research can be a little shocking. The suffering of our ancestors, even though it happened long before we were born, can have deleterious effects on our lives. But this knowledge can also empower us. If we are aware of the environment that shaped our ancestors and the impact it might have had on their biological systems, we have the tools to address whatever negative effects may have been passed on.

Healthy relationships can act as a buffer, allowing the children of parents who suffered traumas to mitigate or outright block the passing on of stress from one generation to another. Knowledge is power. Knowing our ancestral past regarding money can help us learn how to react to our environments in new, potentially more helpful ways.

I want you to take some time and write down as many stories related to money in your family as you can. This can be an ongoing project. You can start by writing down everything you know, and you can continue this practice by asking other people in your family to share their stories. You can keep an ancestral journal or make a visual collage that represents their journey. Let your imagination go wild.

The second part of the practice walks you through using the embodied approach introduced in this book to extend unconditional acceptance to these stories. As you might have guessed, this is not a do-it-once-and-forget-it kind of exercise. This can be an ongoing practice that you make a regular part of your life.

PRACTICE: Unconditionally Accepting Your Ancestral Money Story

Step 1: Find the Stories

Take a moment to scan the stories of your lineage. What anecdotes stand out when it comes to your family and money? What stories were passed on? What was left untold?

Choose one story to work with and take a moment to write out what you remember in your journal. Don't hold back. Allow yourself the permission not to recall exact details. Allow what wants to come through to emerge.

Step 2: Start with Your Heart, Feel the Emotions

When you are done writing, close the computer or put the pen down. Close your eyes and put both of your hands in the center of your chest, close to your heart. Ask yourself what the main emotions are that you feel after telling your ancestral story. See what arises.

Then take some time and let yourself say out loud, "I feel..." Use this phrase as many times as you need until your heart has been heard, understood, and fulfilled.

Step 3: Listen to Your Body, Feel the Energy

With your eyes still closed and your hands on your heart, choose an emotion to work with. Sense the texture of the emotion — its temperature, where it is in your body, and how it feels. See if it has a color and energy associated with it.

Allow that energy to expand while using your breath to keep yourself grounded in your body. Let the energy spread and see the emotion for what it is: energy in motion. If it gets too intense, take a break and open your eyes. Come back to the exercise when you are ready.

Step 4: Turn to Your Mind, Create Some Space

Now let your awareness travel up to your mind center, noticing the energy that lives between your eyes. Ask your mind center to be present, then use your mind to connect the threads between your own experience with money and the familial landscape in which you were raised. Perhaps you see commonalities that feel new. Maybe you want to deepen your awareness of what has always been there. Let the connections intertwine like silk threads in the tapestry of your life. You don't need to fully know the form. Simply allow your personal story and your ancestral story with money to coexist.

Step 5: Offer Unconditional Acceptance, an Embodied Approach

Now choose one moment in your money story that stood out when writing. If you skipped that exercise, instead bring forth a money memory that had an impact on you.

Ask yourself what role lineage plays in your money story. Do not edit what you hear. This is the moment you get to be the person in your lineage who offers up unconditional acceptance for what happened. Remember, acceptance is different from approval. Acceptance acknowledges things as they are, allowing us to cope and face the reality of the situation without resistance. Listen without resistance. Invite the connections to emerge.

As your mind creates insight, bring your awareness back to your heart. This source of unconditional acceptance can aid in updating the energetic state of our nervous system. Use your hands to put pressure on your heart center repeatedly, as if you were pumping waves of unconditional acceptance throughout your body and all its cells.

Breathe in these waves of unconditional acceptance. Let them wash over you as you offer your body physical sensations of love and forgiveness. Unconditional acceptance creates an energetic field in which you can offer your heart, body, and mind the space to accept your lineage without judgment. This creates a new physical reference for your financial DNA. Be with this movement and the showering of unconditional acceptance for as long as you need.

Step 6: Digest, Release, and Integrate

Only when you are ready, release the hands on your heart and open your eyes. Take a moment to breathe in the practice. Pay attention to what feels most present. Is there a familial money pattern that needs to be released? Is there an energy of unconditional acceptance that wants to be digested and integrated?

Take time to choose and either digest or release, however that may look for you. Close this practice by feeling the energy of your ancestors behind you. Even if you have never met them, they are there. Feel into the generations of people who carried your genes and DNA. Know that you are a conduit for helping process their pain so that new futures can be written. Extend a moment of gratitude to yourself and your lineage, and take this sensation of unconditional acceptance with you throughout your day.

Your own unique power of enough can be nurtured through this practice of loving and accepting the challenging stories you have inherited. If you turn away from these familial patterns, they will continue to haunt you. Taking energy, instead of giving energy. But if you can turn toward your financial lineage with an open heart and a connection to mind and body, you can turn your family's old stories into moments of meaning. Unpacking your familial money stories holds important insights to help you find the satisfiers that are appropriate to you and discern which strategies are no longer effective. There are infinite riches to be found on this road to understanding and accepting where you come from.

Healing the Loss of Home

When I think of my own ancestral journey, I am taken to the story of my paternal grandfather, Walter, whom I affectionately called Opa (which means "grandfather" in German). His story is one of loss of home, persecution, war, and scarcity. Yet his story is also one that imbues the resilience of starting over in a foreign land where he didn't know the currency or speak the language. Opa was an Austrian Jew who fled Europe at the age of nineteen at the outbreak of the Second World War. Although driven by the instinctual need for survival, he is also a testament to the perseverance of the human spirit, which knows how to remake itself time and again.

One of my favorite pictures of my grandfather is of him sitting outside his apartment in Bogotá, Colombia, enjoying the open air while sunbathing. He would chase the sun as though he were a sunflower, baking his skin in the warmth of its rays. He looks radiant. And yet this picture was taken with a fence in the background that appears as the outline of a cage, symbolizing the restricted life he lived. He never escaped a deep-seated sense of scarcity. From almost nothing, he was able to remake his life in Bogotá. He became a successful accountant, brought over his remaining family, and reconnected with his teenage love, my grandmother, by writing letters to the Red Cross. She founded one of the first international schools in Bogotá. But despite achieving financial health, stability, and security, Opa never overcame the loss of connection with his homeland or regained a sense of belonging.

Unlike my Opa, my life was full of financial security. I was raised in an upper-middle-class home in New Orleans with professional working parents. My brother and I went to private school, and our parents paid our college tuition in full. We traveled internationally every year to visit family in Colombia and explore the world. I never lacked for anything material, and yet the pain of losing my homeland persisted. At times, the *sense* of scarcity was palpable, which I connected to unprocessed grief. It struck at the core of the question that has captured my focus for more than two decades: Why do we have so much yet feel so poor?

Much like my grandfather lost his homeland, so did my mother. Because my grandfather insisted that my dad pursue a "safer" life, my grandfather stopped at nothing to assure that my father moved to the United States and continued his career in medicine. My father immigrated to a new country to pursue the life he had always dreamed of. While his story taught me the importance of chasing your dreams, my mother's departure from Colombia had a profound impact on my life as well. I was raised to believe that I could do anything, yet I also felt the weight of familial grief.

My mother's loss of home was not due to a violent displacement. It was a choice, though it never felt that way to her. As my father pursued his dream of becoming a doctor in the United

States, my mother's dream of raising our family in Colombia faded. In this way, I inherited a loss of home from both my dad's father and my mother.

The more I listened and learned from the emotions I held, the more I came to understand what had happened to my family. So many of our stories about wealth and money are buried, whether consciously or unconsciously. My grandparents didn't have the tools to turn toward their trauma, and so, quite inadvertently, they passed on their pattern and obsession with financial safety to my dad. He kept us safe and provided everything material I ever needed, while also inspiring me to always pursue my passions and dreams. This gave me a foundation of financial health, purpose, and participation, but it also came at a cost. Anger replaced unprocessed familial grief. Control became my favorite mode of operating in my world, and I was forced to confront some of my greatest financial fears and worst nightmares.

When we use the wisdom of our body, heart, mind, and embodied centers to process information, we become more adept at recognizing how our choices feel in each of our centers. We grow aware of which choices breed a state of scarcity and which enhance a sense of enough.

I have learned that I cannot blame my circumstances when I feel stuck. It is my responsibility to move through whatever challenge I am facing. Sometimes I face the situation with courage and optimism. Other times, I'm met with harder emotions, such as anxiety and dread. Regardless of my reaction, it is my job to see my emotional currency for what it is: a valuable source of information.

Emotions can provide insight, but they aren't the captain of the ship. Instead, when we take the lessons of our money biographies, digest the emotions our memories evoke, and allow for each of our centers to give its perspective, we can wade through the infinite possibilities of choices and discern better alternatives.

We learn from our own mistakes and from those of the people

who have come before us. My parents and grandparents are extremely important people in my life whom I love dearly. Their stories inform and influence me. They are part of my financial and biological DNA. By taking the time to turn toward their stories, I have uncovered valuable insights that have helped me make better choices that align with my current reality.

It wasn't until recently that I understood that the ultimate measure of success wasn't where I lived, but rather what home *felt* like. Home security is not just about safety, protection, stability, and choice. Home security is an embodied security — feeling comfortable and capable of being ourselves, just as we are. Through the power of enough, I have taken the journey to reset the myth of scarcity and give my family a much-needed software update. I am letting go of a way of being in the world that is no longer valid or appropriate. In turn, I am offering this same invitation to you. The stories that got us here won't get us there.

Chapter 10 Takeaways

Integrating Our Personal and Ancestral Financial Histories: Understanding and reconciling one's financial history with one's familial and ancestral money stories is an important step. This deep dive into personal and generational financial narratives enables individuals to recognize patterns, understand their origins, and ultimately, reshape their financial behaviors and outlooks to foster healthier financial habits and beliefs.

The Power of Unconditional Acceptance: The practice of unconditional acceptance is a transformative tool in dealing with financial and emotional challenges rooted in familial and personal histories. By accepting past financial narratives without judgment, individuals can begin to heal from past traumas and make peace with their financial past, which affects their present and future financial decisions and well-being.

Harnessing the Heart's Role in Financial Storytelling: The heart plays an essential role in embracing and expressing vulnerable financial stories. Telling these stories, especially those that reveal financial struggles or hardships, is not just cathartic but crucial for building deeper relationships and developing self-awareness. This process fosters a sense of intimacy and vulnerability, allowing for a more profound connection with others and oneself, which is essential for emotional and financial healing.

Chapter Eleven

ENTERING THE MONEY LIFEWORLD

Money as Embodied Teacher

The power of enough is not an idea but an embodied experience. Your work with unconditional acceptance and money stories can help you to recognize the outlines of a life lived in relationship to profound satiation. But to fully grasp these experiences, you must digest and integrate them into your body. There is no magical pill or simple secret. You can't make the perfect investment or find the ideal job that will finally make you wealthy. Instead, you need to use the tools found in this book. Embodied wealth is a practice that draws on your money story, your wealth mandala, and so many other tools. But when it comes down to it, you must embody the power of enough to fully understand the ongoing sense of well-being that is found through satiation.

Money as an Embodied Teacher

Money is a challenging teacher. It is fun to imagine what you would do if you had an unlimited amount of money. This game might evoke all kinds of ideas, and you might even get a sense of what it feels like to suddenly have millions of dollars. But in reality, these ideas and feelings are not grounded in the reality of your body. Our relationship to money can be very abstract, making it feel confusing, liberating, and infuriating all at once.

233

Grounding your hopes and dreams in the lived experience of your body is exactly the lesson money is trying to teach you. If you haven't lived an experience through your body, it cannot be integrated into your life. Money is a firm mentor and guide, consistently challenging you to turn your dreams into actions. Our relationship with money is a doorway into knowing ourselves.

Money's actual role is to help us work together to create things that would not exist without such complex cooperation. Adopting an embodied approach to life forces you to recognize that the only way to live to the fullest is to work with others. And money is the technology that allows this to happen. It is trying to teach you to embody your dreams by building social currency with everyone around you. If you feel challenged by this statement, take a moment to sit down and have a conversation with money, as we modeled in chapter 3.

Money is a neutral energy that you can learn to wield in life-affirming ways. If you let it, money can be your guide to embodying your dreams. But don't forget that money is just another companion on this journey. It can only do its part, and if you use it to force your will on others, you have already lost the game. Money is your guide and companion. The goal is not to win but to engage with your senses and play with other people.

Listening to the Wisdom of Your Body

We often approach our financial lives through the lens of abstract concepts, mental strategies, and numerical calculations. While these tools are undoubtedly useful and necessary, they can also distance us from a more immediate, embodied understanding of wealth and satiation. To truly transform our relationship with money, we must reconnect with the more primordial wisdom found in the body.

The Austrian-German philosopher Edmund Husserl, my

great-great-uncle on my father's side, described the *lifeworld* as the environment we immediately encounter through daily interactions, prior to any mental filters: "Being an ego through the living body...we are concretely in the field of perception." He argued that we often get stuck in our heads. And even though he wrote in the late nineteenth and early twentieth centuries, his point is still true today. By filtering so much of our experiences through our thoughts and minds, we stay in the realm where we think *about* the world instead of feeling *into* it. When we overemphasize thinking, it comes at the expense of embodied living. It keeps us from vital engagement that is both fulfilling and meaningful. Living an embodied life can remedy our modern malaise of loneliness and isolation.

Husserl offers a practice called *bracketing*. Very simply, bracketing gives us a tool to suspend abstract thought and instead lean toward reality itself, which is our experience of the lifeworld. Here is a straightforward example: Think about someone you care about and the last time you said, "I love you." Feel into the sensations of loving someone. Now bracket the word *love* by taking it out of the equation. The next step is to find other rich, descriptive words that can help you get closer to how you feel. Perhaps you describe your heart bursting out of your chest, or maybe you feel an immense wave of gratitude for this person. Bracket these words. Find new descriptions to take the place of ideas like gratitude. Let these descriptions surface organically, guided and inspired by the sensations you feel in your body, rather than originating from your mind center. This practice of getting behind the words allows you to come closer to the lived experience that language tends to cover up. This is exactly what we mean by suspending preconceived thoughts and allowing what *feels* authentic and true to emerge.

Now, apply this to your relationship to money. Hopefully, the previous practices in the book have helped you clarify your initial thoughts, emotions, and beliefs around money. Take a moment to state in one clear sentence what you feel about money. Maybe you

find yourself saying, "Money, I am grateful for everything you afford me in life," or "Money, I feel uncertain about how you show
up." Take out the key word — in this example, *grateful* or *uncertain* — and revise your description of how you feel about money.
Pause and bring awareness to what sensations start to accompany
your words. It is through these sensations that you guide yourself
back to the lifeworld.

> • MINI MOMENT •
>
> What rich description lies beneath my initial response
> to how I feel about money?
> What does this rich description teach me?

Engaging with Wealth

The lifeworld encompasses our daily activities, relationships, and
sensory experiences in which we are already embedded and engaged. It is the interconnected world where we live together. The
body plays a central role in our experience of this. Through our
senses, the body provides our primary way of knowing and engaging with the world. It allows us to interact with one another and
with nature. The body is not just an object but the very means
through which we experience life. It is by using our body awareness that we can reach below our abstractions to access the source
of well-being and touch our lived experiences directly. Our lived
body gives us access to priceless, intuitive understanding of space,
time, and others.

Understanding the lifeworld and the lived body can have profound implications for your relationship with money. It suggests
that your financial life is not just about numbers and concepts but
also about the qualitative, sensory experiences of vitality, meaning, and satiation. By tuning in to the wisdom of your body, you

can access a deeper, more holistic sense of what true wealth means to you. Your living body is always engaged and interwoven with other bodies. Whereas modern lessons about finance and money leave us feeling isolated and alone, an embodied approach to wealth and well-being is grounded in the knowledge that we are intimately connected to other people and the natural world.

Just as animals move through their environments by instinct and attunement, we, too, can navigate our financial lives with an agility that emerges from our environment. The natural world abounds with rich sensory experiences that evoke a felt sense of abundance and vitality. By bringing this quality of embodied richness into your financial life, you can view wealth as more than just a bunch of numbers in your bank account. Instead, you can access a visceral, life-affirming experience of embodied wealth. It is about the journey itself and how well you live and *sense* it.

Husserl's philosophy, known as phenomenology (emphasizing the direct experience of phenomena), laid the groundwork for later philosophers who developed a more explicit focus on embodiment and the relationship between humans and the natural world. One of the most prominent was Maurice Merleau-Ponty. He shed light on the fact that there is a fundamental reciprocity and intertwining between the body and nature. Just as our bodies shape our perception of the world, the world also shapes our bodily experiences and capacities. For Merleau-Ponty, the body is not a distinct entity but an integral part of the "flesh" of the world — the common, interconnected fabric of being. We matter because we are matter.

In his book *The Spell of the Sensuous*, philosopher David Abram emphasizes the importance of reconnecting with our sensuous, embodied experience of nature to overcome the alienation and disconnection of modern life. He suggests that by cultivating a more direct, participatory relationship with the natural world through our bodily senses, we can regain a sense of belonging and reciprocity with the more-than-human world. Our sensory experience of the environment, mediated by the living body, is the basis for understanding ourselves and our place in the larger ecology. For me, every time I travel to the Amazon I am reminded just how connected I am to the greater web of life.

Phenomenology has contributed to the development of nature-oriented approaches in various fields, including a discipline called somatic psychology that focuses on the role of the body in healing and growth. This tradition recognizes the deep interconnection between human well-being and the health of the natural world. It emphasizes the unity of the soul, mind, heart, and body. Furthermore, it highlights the importance of cultivating embodied, sensory awareness and aligning our lives with the rhythms and wisdom of the living earth. By grounding psychological healing and growth in the context of our embodied relationship with nature, somatic psychology offers a holistic and ecological vision of human flourishing.

It also provides practical tools for cultivating this embodied financial wisdom. Through practices like body awareness, embodied meditation, and somatic release, you can develop a deeper attunement to your bodily experiences regarding money. This is my contribution to you. You can learn to make financial choices not just from mental analysis but from a place of deep, embodied resonance.

• MINI MOMENT •

When do I feel wealthy in my life? What rich, descriptive words best express this?

An Embodied, Somatic Approach to Wealth

As you cultivate this somatic embodied approach to wealth, you may find that your financial life starts to feel more organic and aligned with the natural rhythms of growth and sufficiency. You may discover that true prosperity arises not from accumulating more external wealth but from tending to the richness and vitality of your inner landscapes. By incorporating the wisdom of the lifeworld, the lived body, and the body of the earth into your financial journey, you can embrace a more holistic approach to wealth that encompasses not only monetary gain but also physical well-being, emotional fulfillment, and spiritual connection.

The wisdom of the body is intimately connected to the wisdom of the natural world. After all, our bodies are a microcosm of the earth — made of the same elements, subject to the same cycles and seasons, and imbued with the same life force that animates all living beings. When you attune to your bodily experiences, you connect with your own inner landscape and with the vast intelligence of the ecosystems that sustain us.

Think of the way an animal moves through its environment — with a sense of instinct, attunement, and belonging. There is a naturalness and ease to its movements, a flow that arises from being synchronized with the rhythms of nature. Our human bodies carry this same potential for natural, embodied wisdom. We, too, can learn to move through our financial lives with a sense of natural, grounded agility.

The natural world is also a realm of incredible richness — from the scent of a blooming flower to the warmth of the sun on our skin, from the taste of ripe fruit to the sound of birdsong at dawn. These sensory experiences evoke a felt sense of abundance, pleasure, and vitality. There is an infinite number of meaningful moments available around every corner. When you bring this quality of natural abundance into your relationship with money, you start to experience wealth as a visceral, sensuous experience of life's own power of enough.

At the core of somatic psychology is the idea that the body is a source of a profound intelligence and wisdom. Our physical sensations, postures, and movements can provide valuable insights into our emotional states, beliefs, and patterns of behavior. By learning to listen to and work with these bodily experiences, we can access a deeper level of self-awareness and facilitate powerful changes in our lives.

In the context of transforming our relationship with money, somatic psychology offers a valuable perspective and a set of tools. Your financial experiences and beliefs are not only formed in your mind but are also embodied in your physical reactions and responses. For example, you might feel a tightness in your chest when you think about financial scarcity or bills that need to be paid. Or you may notice a sense of lightness and expansion when you contemplate the more meaningful experiences in your life, when you gift, or when you get paid.

By tuning in to your bodily experiences, you can gain a more nuanced understanding of your relationship with money. You can start to notice how your financial thoughts and emotions manifest in your physical sensations, and how these sensations in turn influence your behaviors and choices. This awareness can help you to identify patterns and obstacles that may hold you back from financial well-being.

Somatic psychology also offers practices for working with the body to facilitate financial transformation. For example, you can use body-based mindfulness practices to cultivate a sense of presence and grounding in the face of financial stress. You can engage in movement exercises to release tension and promote a sense of flow and ease around money. You can also work with bodily postures and gestures to embody qualities like confidence, openness, and abundance.

Integrating somatic psychology into the process of transforming our relationship with money can powerfully deepen our self-awareness, release limiting patterns, and cultivate a more embodied sense of financial well-being. By listening to the wisdom of our bodies and working with our physical experiences, we can create a more holistic and sustainable approach to wealth and prosperity.

Below are some key principles and practices from somatic psychology that can be applied to financial transformation. As you read through them, see if you can connect to situations in your financial life where they could be useful.

- **Body Awareness:** Your journey into the vitality of the lifeworld begins by bringing your awareness to the life of your body. Developing a deep and nuanced awareness of your physical sensations, movements, and responses related to money is an important first step on your journey to embodied wealth and satiation.

- **Embodied Meditation:** Meditation can take various forms beyond sitting on a cushion or walking in silence. It can also involve contact with another human or the natural world. Some examples include meditating while in physical contact with a partner, back-to-back. Or having someone sit behind you and place their hand in the center of your back to connect your body with your heart. This physical contact can help awaken senses and keep you present in the moment. Or spending time in nature, allowing your senses to be fully present and taking stock of what you see, hear, smell, and feel. This leads to practicing presence and nonjudgmental attention to our bodily experiences around financial situations.

- **Somatic Release:** Somatic release is crucial to living a vital life. Your body holds on to trauma, stress, and tension. It learns certain habits to cope with the world, but not all of these are beneficial. As part of the digestion process introduced earlier in this book, we talked about the need for elimination. In the context of the body, this can look like physical release. Using movement, breath, and touch, you can release physical tension and emotional blocks related to money.

241

- **Somatic Integration:** Somatic integration is equally important as release. Circling back to the practice of digesting meaningful experiences, your body becomes the vessel that invites you to slow down and breathe during your most important and profound moments. As with release, you can use movement, breath, and touch to integrate vital moments that you experience, contributing to your own deep well of satiation.

- **Vital Movements:** I cannot stress this one enough. It is crucial that you find some activity or movement that feeds your body. This can include anything from dance and yoga to hiking and any number of sports. Whatever it is for you, find those activities that make you feel agile and vital and incorporate them into your daily routine. Explore how your bodily postures and gestures reflect your financial beliefs and attitudes, and experiment with new postures to embody positive financial qualities.

- **Embodied Art and Metaphor:** Our bodies tend to process things in a nonverbal manner. Discovering activities and practices that are beneficial for you is essential. But I have found that it is also helpful to use art and metaphor to process and express the insights you glean from your embodied experience. This can include painting, playing music, and writing. And it is important to note that these artistic expressions do not need to meet any quality standards. It can be incredibly helpful just to pull out crayons and create drawings, just like you did when you were a child. Exploring your insights through art and metaphor can help you to reflect on your stories about money and discover the various ways you might revitalize your approach to embodied wealth.

- **Somatic Resourcing:** We all need to feel safe and secure in both our lives and our bodies. Resourcing is the practice of attuning into the sensations that help you feel grounded. You can close your eyes and imagine yourself in a place you naturally feel secure and calm. Let your body stay there until you feel a deep sense of serenity. It is important that you spend time learning the places where you feel most secure, as well as the places where you feel most alive. The contexts in which your body thrives matter. Cultivate a felt sense of safety, support, and resilience in the body to navigate financial challenges with greater ease.

- **Embodied Play:** Last but certainly not least, you need to remember to play. Your body is your direct connection to an abundance of energy that flows through the world. It is easy to forget this as we age, so it is of utmost importance that you include time for play to encourage an ongoing experience of vitality in your life. Play is essential for cognitive, emotional, and social development, enhancing skills such as problem-solving, empathy, and communication. It provides significant benefits for reducing stress and improving physical health. Adding play to your life, however that looks, will help build bonds, enhance a sense of belonging, and foster creative ways to improve your well-being.

Incorporating these somatic principles and practices can deepen your financial transformation, helping you tap into a deeper level of wisdom and intelligence. You can learn to trust the guidance of your body and align your financial choices with your deepest values and needs by paying attention to valuable information gathered through your senses. Ultimately, this embodied approach to wealth can help you create a more fulfilling sense of richness that encompasses not just financial health but also physical vitality and embodied security.

• MINI MOMENT •

Which of these somatic practices is always easily available to me?

PRACTICE: A Journey to Embodied Wealth

This exercise is designed to help you integrate the principles of embodied wealth and begin cultivating a more holistic, somatic relationship with wealth and money.

Step 1: Body Awareness

Begin by choosing a comfortable seated or lying position. You can do this in your home or find a place in nature that calls to you.

Once you have found the right place, take a few deep breaths and bring your awareness to your physical body. Scan your body from head to toe, noticing any areas of tension or discomfort. As you go through this body scan, you may also want to pay special attention to areas you associate with your body, heart, mind, or even your soul. Don't get stuck in definitions. Just allow yourself to be surprised if some area of your body feels like it is more aligned with one of these centers.

See if there are any places that catch your interest or make you feel curious. Take your time with this part of the exercise. If you are drawn to any part of your body, take note of it and simply be aware of any physical sensations without passing any judgment. Find rich, descriptive words to express these sensations. You are welcome to say them out loud.

Now, take a moment to think of your relationship to money. You have done a lot of work to outline your stories about money. See if anything jumps out as you open yourself to all the habits, patterns, experiences, and insights you have had about money, both while reading this book and in your life.

Once you have a specific experience that you would like to focus on, see if you can feel where it is located in your body. Notice any physical sensations, emotions, or bodily responses that arise when you think about money, wealth, or your current financial situation. Again, don't get lost in trying to do this right. Allow yourself to be surprised by what shows up and where it manifests in your body.

Where do you feel these sensations in your body?

What emotions or beliefs are associated with them?

What colors, images, or symbols are connected to this experience?

Don't let your imagination wander too far. Keep your attention focused on your body. Just be curious about what shows up in relation to your money story. Once you have a sense of the specific experience that is most alive for you and where it is in your body, place your hands on that area and take a deep breath.

Step 2: Embodied Meditation

Now that you have a sense of the specific experience that is most alive for you and where it is in your body, I invite you to do an embodied meditation. We usually associate meditation with sitting on a cushion and developing a sense of mindfulness. While these practices can help you in an embodied meditation, we are going to undertake something a little different. You can do one of three things.

Practice Solo

First, you can do the meditation on your own. Keep your hand on the place where your experience is in your body.

Bring your attention to the area and focus on making contact with it. Allow the contact to amplify or deepen what you are already feeling, then let yourself be surprised by what wants to be seen and felt. You can choose to do this within a set amount of time, or simply allow the practice to organically unfold on its own.

Once the meditation is over, take some time to draw, write, move, or express what has shown up. This practice of embodied art allows whatever insights or memories want to come to the surface to become more concrete.

Practice with an Object

A second form of the practice involves choosing an object from your house or from the natural environment. If you take this route, connect with the experience in your body, then walk around wherever you happen to be to see if some object catches your attention.

Spend a few moments observing it with all your senses — its texture, color, weight, temperature, and any other qualities you notice. As you connect with this object, imagine that it represents your relationship with wealth. Once you have a sense of the object and its significance, follow the same format as for the solo option above, placing the object rather than your hand in contact with the area of your body where you feel the strongest connection to money.

As the meditation ends, make sure to take time to express any insights or memories in an artistic, somatic, or nonverbal way.

Practice with Another

There is a third option that is also available, which is to find another person to engage with. If you take this route, you can either bring them up to speed by inviting them to connect with their own money story, or you can simply ask for their help.

Once you are ready, ask the person to put their hand on the part of your body where you experience your relationship with money. Depending on what feels most appropriate, you might also ask them to make contact in some other way. For instance, you could sit back-to-back with them, or they could rest their head on your shoulder. Or they might place their hand in the center of your back. The crucial part is that the other person is in direct physical contact with your body where the money experience is most pronounced. The contact they offer should be steady. This is not bodywork or a massage. Their physical contact is meant to provide a grounding sense of presence with another physical body, which can help your mind and heart stay rooted and focused on sensation.

Once you have found an appropriate way to create this physical connection, follow the guidance above. Throughout this process, you will need to both release and integrate certain feelings and experiences by digesting them and then allowing them to move through your body.

Step 3: Somatic (Embodied) Release

We store all kinds of memories and experiences in the body. Many of these have felt overwhelming for some reason and have not been digested. When we move away from such experiences, trying not to feel them, they can get stuck in our bodies, creating energetic blocks, which I think of as hot spots. It is of the utmost importance that you find ways to move these experiences through your body.

In the practices above, if you found places that were especially hot, sore, or maybe even a little stuck or rigid. These are good candidates for somatic release. To release these block-ages, you may want to do one of two things. First, it may help to bring your full attention to the area. See what images or feelings are present and, to the extent that it feels useful, lean into them. You do need to be mindful here. The point is not to get stuck in the patterns that are present but to feel them so that they can move through. Adding touch and massage can also be beneficial. You can do this for yourself, and you can also seek assistance from a friend or a professional who works in the realm of somatic healing.

The second approach focuses more on movement. Your body has an innate ability to digest and heal unprocessed ex-periences. Depending on the experience, the energy stuck in your body may be either integrated or eliminated. There is a subtle art to this process, but the wisdom of your body is capable of guiding you through digesting old challenges and traumas. To nurture a somatic release, focus on the specific place in your body where there seems to be a blockage. Stay with the experience to see what movement or release wants to happen.

You may wish to rise and allow your body to move in any way that feels natural and expressive. Let the sensations, emo-tions, or beliefs you noticed in the previous steps guide your movements. If you feel tension or constriction, let your move-ments release and soften those areas. If you feel a sense of ease or expansion, amplify those qualities through your move-ments. As you move, you may also choose to vocalize or make sounds that resonate with your experience. Allow your body to express itself freely, without judgment or censorship. Be open to what shows up, and at every step of the way, lean into the natural wisdom of your body.

For those who are struggling to move through some ex-perience on their own, there are many modalities that can be helpful. In his groundbreaking book *Waking the Tiger*, Peter Levine introduced the concept of somatic experiencing, a therapeutic approach that emphasizes the body's innate ability to heal from trauma through completing physiological responses that were halted during traumatic events. He promotes gently guiding clients to become aware of their body sensations and using techniques such as titration and pendulation to safely work through and release any trapped traumatic energy.

Step 4: Somatic (Embodied) Integration

The process of somatic integration is the key to your ongoing sense of vitality and creativity. Similar to the process of somatic release in step 3, you will find that numerous experiences are longing to be integrated into your body. This is the fundamental ground on which your sense of satiation is built. To fully embody the power of enough, you must digest the profound and meaningful experiences in your life. Take a moment to physically swallow whatever insights emerge.

The goal is to integrate sensations of vitality (body), feelings of intimacy (heart), and visions of growth (mind) while opening to the emergence of meaning (soul). Allow yourself to be surprised and follow your natural flow toward digesting and integrating the meaningful experiences that are part of your money story. Notice how it feels in your body. Where do you sense vitality, joy, or aliveness? Breathe into those sensations, allowing them to expand and integrate into your being.

This part of the process is fundamental to your ongoing embodiment of wealth. We all have amazing experiences. These can be subtle, intimate connections that happen between you and a loved one, and they can be connected to once-in-a-lifetime experiences that inspire awe and wonder. Either way, the goal is to feel these meaningful experiences, so that you can integrate them into your newly embodied "bank" account — your unique power of enough.

Step 5: Commitment and Consistency

In any book on habit formation, coaching, or personal growth, you will find that one of the most important parts of any transformative process is the commitment to the goal, followed by consistent and ongoing practice to achieve that goal.

Spend a few moments reflecting on your experience with this exercise. What insights or realizations did you gain about your relationship with money and embodied wealth?

Identify one specific action or practice you can commit to incorporating into your daily life to cultivate a more embodied and somatic approach to financial well-being. This could be a regular satiation journal practice, mindful time in nature, a meaningful CW$, or any other activity that resonates with you. Write down your commitment and place it in a prominent location as a reminder to yourself.

Remember, embodied wealth is an ongoing journey of self-discovery, presence, and alignment with your deepest values and aspirations. It requires both commitment and consistency. By engaging with these practices regularly, you can deepen your connection to the power of enough and create a life of true prosperity and fulfillment.

It goes without saying, but embodied wealth is not a destination. There is no retirement from life. No amount of money you save will enable you to finally check that item off your list. A life lived in connection with the power of enough is an ongoing journey, one that asks you to continue to embody the wealth of your meaningful experiences. The pursuit of embodied wealth never ends. No conclusions. No final mountains to climb, skills to gain, or people to meet. No amount of money will get you there, and yet money is such an incredible guide. The experiences you have processed and released through somatic integration can be added to the bigger picture of your life. Go back out there and enjoy the process of living your fullest life as you rinse, satiate, and repeat.

Chapter 11 Takeaways

The Lifeworld of Wealth: Embodied wealth is about cultivating a visceral, sensory experience of abundance and vitality, not just accumulating money or possessions. True wealth arises from aligning your financial life with the wisdom of your body, your connection to the natural world, and a felt sense of profound satiation.

Somatic Psychology: Somatic psychology and an embodied approach offer powerful tools for transforming your relationship with money, such as body awareness, embodied meditation, somatic release, and integrating meaningful experiences. These practices help you become more attuned to your bodily sensations around money and make choices from a place of grounded presence.

Mind-Heart-Body-Soul Alignment: True embodied wealth arises from aligning your mind, heart, body, and soul around money. Work with your mindset, regulate your financial emotions, develop aligned habits and behaviors, and stay connected to your deepest values and life purpose. An integrated mind-heart-body-soul approach unlocks embodied wealth.

CONCLUSION

Embodied Wealth, a Path Toward
the Power of Enough

In today's world, the pursuit of financial success often overshadows the importance of health and well-being. You were taught to believe that wealth is measured by the size of your bank accounts, the material possessions you own, and the status symbols you acquire. However, this narrow definition of wealth can leave you feeling disconnected, unfulfilled, and trapped in an abundance-scarcity cycle of endless striving.

In this book, wealth has been redefined to encompass not just financial abundance, but also the richness of our intimate relationships, the vitality of our bodies, the depth of our personal growth, and the sense of meaning and purpose in our lives. As you engage in life at these levels, you find yourself organically aligned with your soul.

The path to enoughness *includes* money as an important mirror and an invaluable guide. Too often, we see money as an impediment or scapegoat on this journey, either hoarding or rejecting it. Money is a social technology that empowers us with agency. When we take a moment to pause and reflect on the actions and outcomes of our financial past, we can learn to refine our future decisions, making them more aligned with our personal goals and values. It is here that money has an important role to play.

To connect with your soul's purpose, you need to cultivate a relationship with money that is grounded in satiation and in alignment with your deepest values. This is the power of enough. By working with all aspects of our being — soul, mind, heart, and body — we can create a holistic and sustainable sense of wealth that supports us in living our best lives. Our conscious and unconscious beliefs about money shape our emotional responses to financial situations, which ultimately influence our behaviors and choices. By examining and transforming our money mindset, we can create a ripple effect that positively affects our financial habits and outcomes.

The mind is a powerful tool in this process. Our thoughts and beliefs about money often stem from our early experiences, family narratives, and societal conditioning. We can get stuck in mental models that limit our financial potential and keep us stuck in patterns of scarcity, fear, or overspending. But the mind also has the power to take a step back, offering us a chance to see any number of possibilities on the horizon. The mind can also align with constructive archetypes — crowdsourced patterns of possibility that allow us to draw on the collective wisdom of our ancestors.

But the mind alone is not enough. The life of the heart, and the emotions that come along with it, play an important role in your journey. By embracing vulnerability and seeking intimacy, we can rest in the heart's experiences of connection and belonging. And with connection comes overlapping and overwhelming interactions that can create a veritable flood of emotions. If we are going to uncover the riches available through intimate connection, then we must learn to embody and digest what we are feeling. The heart can be overwhelmed by joy, love, and desire, as well as fear, anxiety, shame, and guilt.

These are all common emotional responses to financial and life challenges alike. They can cloud our judgment and lead us to make reactive, short-sighted decisions. And yet the heart has the secret ability to offer unconditional acceptance. As we develop emotional intelligence, we can expand our ability to be with strong emotions when it comes to our stories about money. As the heart and money learn to work together, they can teach us to recognize and regulate our financial emotions in healthy ways. By cultivating and embodying positive emotional states like gratitude, abundance, and contentment, we can shift our financial energy and attract more opportunities for growth and success.

But the heart and mind together are not enough. If you want to embody wealth, you must recognize the importance of taking consistent action aligned with the wisdom of your body and your financial goals. Your behaviors and habits around money are bodily expressions of your thoughts and emotions. In this way, your experience of our shared lifeworld has a direct impact on your financial well-being. By developing new, purposeful actions aimed at embodying wealth as defined in these pages, you can create lasting change and abundance in your life.

An embodied approach to wealth ensures holistic financial transformation. As you integrate your experiences of the mind, heart, and body, this creates a connection to a deeper sense of meaning found in the soul. Rather than focusing solely on budgeting, saving, or investing strategies, this model addresses the more profound psychological and emotional factors that shape our relationship with money. It recognizes that true financial wealth is not just about accumulating more scarce resources but about cultivating a sense of vitality, intimacy, purpose, satiation, and alignment with your soul's connection to your power of enough. And in this journey, money is a trusted friend.

True Wealth Is Cultivated from Within

At the heart of this journey is the recognition that true wealth is cultivated from within. By tapping into the power of enough and learning to embody the experiences of abundance, vitality, intimacy, growth, and satiation, you create an unshakable foundation of enoughness that will support you in navigating life's challenges and opportunities with grace and resilience.

Remember that the journey of embodied wealth is ongoing. It requires a commitment to self-discovery, growth, and alignment as well as a willingness to embrace the wisdom of our whole being — mind, heart, body, and soul.

The following, final practice is a powerful way to integrate the key principles and insights from this book into your daily life. By creating a sacred space for self-discovery, awakening your bodily wisdom, harnessing your emotional intelligence, embracing a growth mindset, connecting with your soul's purpose, and taking inspired action, you can deepen your relationship with money and create a financial reality that reflects your deepest values and aspirations.

As you engage in this practice and continue your journey of embodied wealth, trust in the power of your own wisdom and the richness of the universe to support you. Remember that you are the creator of your own financial story. By aligning your money with your authentic self and your most remarkable vision for your life, you become a powerful force for positive change in the world.

So, let us step forward into this final practice with courage, curiosity, and an open heart, knowing that the path of embodied wealth is one of endless growth, discovery, and possibility. May this journey bring you ever closer to the life of true prosperity, purpose, and joy that you so richly deserve.

PRACTICE: Reclaiming Your Financial Agency

Wealth isn't something we acquire from the outside but something we cultivate from within. By tapping into the wisdom of our bodies, hearts, minds, and souls, we reclaim our financial agency and create a relationship with money that truly nourishes and empowers us. This is the essence of this practice — a transformative journey of self-discovery and alignment that invites you to connect with your deepest values, unique gifts, and innate power to create a financial reality that supports your highest vision for your life and the world. As you embody your financial power and make choices that honor your whole being, you'll discover that true wealth is not just about what you have. It is also about who you are and the impact you make on the world around you.

Step 1: Create a Sacred Space for Self-Discovery

Carve out dedicated time and find a peaceful place where you can turn inward and explore all the lessons this book helped you learn about your relationship with money. Take a few grounding breaths and connect with your intention to reclaim your financial agency.

Step 2: Awaken Your Bodily Wisdom

Bring your awareness to your physical sensations and energy levels. Ask your body what it needs to feel vibrant, healthy, and empowered. Listen deeply to its wisdom and consider how you can make financial choices that honor its needs and support your overall well-being.

Step 3: Tap Into Your Emotional Intelligence

Allow yourself to acknowledge and feel the full spectrum of emotions that arise when you contemplate your financial life. Embrace your emotional responses as valuable messengers that can guide you toward more authentic and fulfilling choices. Ask yourself how you can use your financial resources to cultivate more love, joy, and connection in your life and relationships.

Step 4: Harness the Power of Your Mind

Observe your thoughts and beliefs around money with curiosity and compassion. Challenge any limiting beliefs or self-defeating patterns that may be undermining your financial agency. If you get stuck, remember to use the conversation with money tool (chapter 3). Money is ready to engage. Embrace a growth mindset that sees challenges as opportunities for learning and transformation. Set empowering financial goals that align with your values and dreams.

Step 5: Connect with Your Soul's Purpose

Reflect on your deepest values, your unique gifts, and the impact you want to make in the world. Ask yourself how you can align your financial choices with your soul's calling and use your resources to create more meaning, beauty, and goodness in the world. Trust in your soul's guidance and let it inspire you to make brave and purposeful choices.

Step 6: Craft Your Personalized Action Plan

Based on the insights you've gained from tuning in to your body, heart, and mind and their connection to your soul, identify specific steps to reclaim your financial agency and align your money with your deepest values and aspirations. What needs require attention? What satisfiers can be amplified or changed? Break down your goals into manageable tasks that you can focus on within the next twelve months. Celebrate each small victory along the way. In the words of one of my teachers, Carolyn Buck Luce, focus on the next move that is totally possible today but holds a hint of the future dream. A "tiny mighty" move. From that new step, the next set of possibilities emerges.

Step 7: Embody Your Financial Power

Stay connected to your intention of being an empowered and conscious steward of your financial resources as you go about your daily life. Notice when old patterns or beliefs arise and gently realign yourself with your new, empowering money story. Take inspired action and trust in your ability to create a financial reality that serves and sustains you.

By embodying wealth, you reclaim your financial agency and step into your power as the creator of your financial reality. You learn to trust the wisdom of your body, heart, mind, and soul to make financial choices that honor your whole being. As you align your money with your deepest values and aspirations, you experience a profound sense of freedom, purpose, and abundance that radiates into every area of your life. You become a sovereign cocreator of a world where wealth is measured not just in dollars but in the richness of your connections, the depth of your experiences, and the impact you make on the world around you.

As you complete this practice, take a moment to appreciate the profound transformation that is available to you by turning toward the wisdom of your natural embodied sense of wealth and well-being. By engaging in this powerful journey of self-discovery and alignment, you can take significant steps toward creating a life of true joy, grounded in an infinite portfolio comprised of compounded moments of meaning.

I truly hope this book helps you awaken to the truth that wealth is about not just financial resources but also the richness of your experiences, the depth of your relationships, and the impact you make in the world. If you take away only a few things, I hope they include a newfound trust in the wisdom of your body, heart, mind, and soul; some practical tools to make financial choices that honor your whole being; and a nuanced understanding that money is an important teacher, guide, and friend.

As you move forward, remember that you possess the power to create a financial reality that reflects your deepest values and greatest aspirations. You were never bound by scarcity, fear, or comparison. That was just a tired story that we would all be better to leave behind. Integrate these into your life and embrace the infinite possibilities that arise as you continue learning how to embody enough.

The journey toward embodied wealth is an ongoing one, filled with endless opportunities for learning, discovery, and transformation. By staying connected to your deepest values and trusting in your own inner wisdom, you can navigate the complexities of your financial life with clarity and purpose.

Remember, too, that you are not alone on this path. Sharing your experiences and insights with others makes you part of a community that is redefining wealth and creating a new paradigm of satiation and joy. As you continue to cultivate a relationship with money grounded in moments of meaning, you'll find that your financial journey becomes a powerful catalyst for positive change — not just in your own life but in the lives of those around you.

I hope you have found something in these pages that allows you to move forward with confidence and purpose. Every choice you make is an opportunity to create a financial reality that serves and sustains you. Listen to all your centers, encouraging them to learn from one another. This should open you to new possibilities that emerge when every aspect of yourself is involved in a continuous collaboration.

Talk to money often and teach this practice to your kids. I aspire to live in a world where money isn't feared or hoarded but treated as an important guide.

The power to create a life of true wealth and satiation lies within you. By staying connected to your authentic self and your deepest aspirations, you'll find that the journey of embodied wealth is one of endless growth, discovery, and fulfillment, leading you to uncover the power of enough.

ACKNOWLEDGMENTS

First and foremost, my gratitude and deep sense of partnership and satiation go to my husband, Zayin. This book would not have been birthed without you. We have added one more member to our family. I love my life with you. Ixchel, you are named after the moon goddess of becoming, and as my daughter, you remind me daily that we are constantly evolving and can't be boxed in. I love your courage, perseverance, and joy for life. Mami and Papi, there are no words to describe the support, love, and commitment you each have given me. I am proud of who I am because of you. Alex, you taught me how to laugh and not take myself too seriously. To the rest of my family, I send so much love and gratitude for your unwavering support and encouragement. I love you all so deeply and even more, the way we celebrate life together. I am proud of who we are. This book is for those who came before us.

Bridget Boland, my book coach and midwife, thank you for helping me reach publication and for showing me that success is not just measured by book sales but also by receiving an enthusiastic standing ovation for saying what needed to be said. Melanie Abrams, thank you for guiding my publishing path. You've inspired me since I met you. Laura Mazer, you gave me a wholehearted *yes* when I most needed it, and you continue to guide me beautifully. Best book agent ever! Georgia Hughes, you reminded me that I was ahead of the game and helped me pace my journey. I am so grateful for your decades of experience and your ability to recognize that my delivery system has a place in the world. To the team at New World Library, including Monique Muhlenkamp, Tona Pearce Myers, Tracy Cunningham, and Kristen Cashman, thank you for making my dream a reality. Addison Gilligan and the PR team at Fortier, you helped breathe life into the promotion of this book in ways I could never have imagined. Your passion and enthusiasm are contagious! Angela Knapik, Brooke and Rachel Latham, and the team of Social Canvas, your beautifully crafted digital message speaks louder than words. I feel so grateful to have you as part of my team. Caitlin Lang, I love my website and cover art! You captured my essence fully, and it shows. Patricia, you have kept me humble, open, and human in this process. Thank you for being a guide and ground to stand on.

Lynne Twist, Sara Vetter, and Carolyn Buck Luce — you each gave me the final push across the finish line when I most needed it and inspire me to be my most remarkable shining star. Lynne, your inspiration goes beyond words. I am so grateful for your work and how you walk in this world. Thank you for saying yes. I feel seen. Carolyn, you helped me touch what is longing to happen and claim it as my own.

To all those who came to my fortieth birthday party to hear me declare out loud that I was committing to this book, thank you for contributing to my success, showing up with words of encouragement and appreciation, and dancing the night away. I remember that commitment often, and I hold you each in my heart by name.

To my ritual mamas (Emily, Sage, Manisha, Savitha, Vinitha, Jahbi, Cornelia, Vere, Paula, Rachel, Shannon, Erica, Abby, and Hanna), you keep me connected to magic — our circles and connections fill me up. My last birthday circle was exactly what I needed to cross the finish line. To my pod ritual mamas (Geralyn, Cristina, and Jamie), I satiated my need for belonging with you. No words, just sheer gratitude. Kara, Cate, Michael, David T., you have held and loved me dearly from afar. I feel you always. Jimena, forever a sister no matter the distance. Krista, your depth and constant companionship on my book journey are forever lodged in my heart. Jorge, Coby, Jackie, Whitney, Emma, Kerri, Skylar, Ixone, Aninha, Steve, Brandon, Ty, Arian, Sam, Lisa, and Ryan, you cheered me on until the very end. Rachel Kaplan — I love sharing the NWL journey with you! Bravo and well done! Tzaddi, Sarah, and Emilie, you are true family and the first outside readers that made me feel I actually had something to contribute. I am so grateful, and I can't wait to be a guest speaker at your book clubs!

To all the communities I have been part of (Elmwood, Malidoma, West Coast Village, HS, CIIS, 1024/1028, Remarkable Women, Dancing Queens, Sophia Sisters, Park Day 2024 Parent Cohort), I walk in the world with a deep sense of security because I know each of you has my back. I never thought community living would shape me so deeply. Marina, Ramon, and Jorge, you opened a world I never imagined possible by inviting me to dive into all of me through my centers. Your work lives on in this book.

To my family at Peak360, you proved that my two values of depth and wealth can coexist. Thank you for letting me be a thought leader in our field and saying yes to our culture of leaning in. Pat, Samson, and Andy — I wouldn't walk this path with anyone else. We have one another's back. Andrea, your daily support and generosity of spirit go beyond words. Hands down, this book is finished because of your dedication to my practice, keeping me focused, on task, and afloat. Thank you! To my clients, you have supported me every step of the way, honoring my much-needed out-of-office Fridays so that I could write. So much of the inspiration for this book comes from what you've shared. I cherish your money stories as if they were my own. It is an honor to be a trusted advisor in your life.

Finally, to my ancestors: I dedicate this book to you. May you be fed with our hearts, bodies, minds, and spirits. I feel your standing ovation. I could not have written this book without you.

NOTES

Chapter 1: Redefining Wealth

p. 15 *economics has been defined as the study of human behavior*: Lionel Robbins, *An Essay on the Nature and Significance of Economic Science* (London: Macmillan and Co., 1932), 15.

p. 15 *wealth is the accumulation of scarce resources*: *Oxford English Dictionary*, 2nd ed. (2004), s.v. "wealth."

p. 16 *Wallace D. Wattles*: Wallace D. Wattles, *The Science of Getting Rich* (Holyoke, MA: Elizabeth Towne Company, 1910).

p. 16 *Napoleon Hill*: Napoleon Hill, *Think and Grow Rich* (Meriden, CT: Ralston Society, 1937).

p. 16 abundance mindset *was coined by Stephen R. Covey*: Stephen R. Covey, *The 7 Habits of Highly Effective People: Restoring the Character Ethic* (New York: Free Press, 1989).

p. 18 finite *and* infinite *games*: James P. Carse, *Finite and Infinite Games* (New York: Free Press, 1986). Simon Sinek popularized Carse's work when he applied this theory to organizational development in his recent book *The Infinite Game* (New York: Penguin, 2019).

p. 23 *"What you appreciate, appreciates"*: Lynne Twist, *The Soul of Money: Transforming Your Relationship with Money and Life* (New York: Norton, 2003), 120.

Chapter 2: Redefining Money

p. 31 *"money is the most universally motivating"*: Lynne Twist, *The Soul of Money: Transforming Your Relationship with Money and Life* (New York: Norton, 2003), 7.

p. 32   *Money has four main functions*: Aristotle, *Nicomachean Ethics* 3.5; Aristotle, *Politics* 1.8–10.

p. 33   *shell necklaces may have been used as money*: Mikael Fauvelle, *Shell Money: A Comparative Study* (Cambridge: Cambridge University Press, 2024), 60–61.

p. 34   *Money is a* social technology: Fauvelle, *Shell Money*, 7–9. See also Michael Peneder, "Digitization and the Evolution of Money as a Social Technology of Account," *Journal of Evolutionary Economics* 32, no. 1 (2022): 175–203; and Sebastian Felten, *Money in the Dutch Republic: Everyday Practice and Circuits of Exchange* (Cambridge: Cambridge University Press, 2022).

p. 34   *pieces of paper called* redes de trueque: Georgina M. Gómez, "Money as an Institution: Rule versus Evolved Practice? Analysis of Multiple Currencies in Argentina," *Journal of Risk and Financial Management* 12, no. 2 (2019): 7–8.

p. 34   *six hundred alternative currencies*: Garrick Hileman, "Alternative Currencies: A Historical Survey and Taxonomy," SSRN, March 1, 2013, 28.

p. 35   *"he/she/it believes"*: *Credunt* is the Latin word that would be used for "they believe."

p. 38   *"Barter economies rarely existed"*: Fauvelle, *Shell Money*, 1–2.

p. 43   *"We are not wired to enjoy things"*: Michael Easter, *Scarcity Brain: Fix Your Craving Mindset and Rewire Your Habits to Thrive with Enough* (New York: Rodale / Random House, 2023). See chapters on "Influence," "Food," and "Stuff."

p. 43   *"scarcity cues"*: Easter, *Scarcity Brain*, 3.

p. 44   *"scientists now call this 'brand tribalism'"*: Easter, *Scarcity Brain*, 179.

p. 45   *"Modern capitalism is a pro at two things"*: Morgan Housel, *The Psychology of Money: Timeless Lessons on Wealth, Greed, and Happiness* (Hampshire, UK: Harriman House, 2020), 41.

Chapter 3: Conversations with Money

p. 53   *the chemistry of an emotion*: Jill Bolte Taylor, *Whole Brain Living: The Anatomy of Choice and the Four Characters That Drive Our Life* (Carlsbad, CA: Hay House, 2021), 7.

p. 54   *the intricate workings of our brains' emotional processing*: Taylor, *Whole Brain Living*, 7.

Chapter 4: Dialogue as Currency

p. 71 *"thinking win-win"*: Stephen R. Covey, *The 7 Habits of Highly Effective People: Restoring the Character Ethic* (New York: Free Press, 1989), 231.

p. 73 *more money does not necessarily enhance happiness*: S. R. Yates, "Money Can't Buy Happiness... or Can It?," *Journal of Financial Education* 46, no. 2 (2020): 331–43.

Chapter 6: Recognizing That Needs Are Natural

p. 112 *"integrated wholeness of the organism"*: A. H. Maslow, "A Theory of Human Motivation," *Psychological Review* 50, no. 4 (1943): 370.

p. 113 *"enable people to become healthy"*: A. H. Maslow, "Critique of Self-Actualization Theory," *Journal of Humanistic Education and Development* 29, no. 3 (1991): 104.

p. 113 *a management consultant firm reimagined Maslow's theory*: Scott Barry Kaufman, *Transcend: The New Science of Self-Actualization* (New York: TarcherPerigee, 2020).

p. 114 *a state of growth and becoming*: A. H. Maslow, *Toward a Psychology of Being* (New York: Van Nostrand, 1968), 23.

p. 114 *One out of every seven adults*: Neli Esipova, Julie Ray, and Ying Han, "750 Million Struggling to Meet Basic Needs with No Safety Net," *Gallup*, June 16, 2020, https://news.gallup.com/poll/312401/750 -million-struggling-meet-basic-needs-no-safety-net.aspx.

p. 115 *"inner core"*: Maslow, *Toward a Psychology of Being*, 158.

p. 115 *"becoming ceases for a moment"*: Maslow, *Toward a Psychology of Being*, 176.

p. 116 *the way we satisfy these needs differs*: Maslow's work has been critiqued for being too Euro American. "There is a common misconception that Maslow's theory didn't allow for cross-cultural variation or individual differences. However, Maslow acknowledged that not only can our basic needs ebb and flow in salience across a person's lifetime, but there can also be significant cultural and individual differences in the order in which people satisfy their basic needs" (Kaufman, *Transcend*, xxix).

p. 116 *He called the strategies we use*: Antonio Elizalde, Manfred Max-Neef, and Martín Hopenhayn, *Human Scale Development: Conception, Application and Further Reflections* (London: Apex Press, 1991).

Chapter 7: Creating Your Wealth Mandala

p. 148 *"superpower of superpowers"*: Rick Hanson, *Hardwiring Happiness: The New Brain Science of Contentment, Calm, and Confidence* (New York: Harmony Press, 2016), 50.

p. 157 *we truly become adults*: Bill Plotkin, *Nature and the Human Soul: Cultivating Wholeness and Community in a Fragmented World* (Novato, CA: New World Library, 2010).

p. 161 *"We often resist what we need most"*: Julia Cameron, *The Artist's Way* (New York: Penguin, 2002).

Chapter 8: What Is Enough?

p. 182 *This involves recognizing our limits*: Pooja Lakshmin, *Real Self-Care: A Transformative Program for Redefining Wellness (Crystals, Cleanses, and Bubble Baths Not Included)* (London: Penguin, 2023).

p. 183 *"Pain is inevitable"*: Haruki Murakami, *What I Talk about When I Talk about Running: A Memoir* (New York: Knopf Doubleday, 2009), vii.

Chapter 9: Writing Your Money Story

p. 197 *our ability to create and share myths and stories*: Jonathan Gottschall, *The Storytelling Animal: How Stories Make Us Human* (London: Houghton Mifflin Harcourt, 2012).

p. 197 *"money isn't a material reality"*: Yuval Noah Harari, *Sapiens: A Brief History of Humankind*, quoted in Gottschall, *The Storytelling Animal*, 179.

p. 197 *"money is the most universal"*: Harari, *Sapiens*, quoted in Gottschall, *The Storytelling Animal*, 179.

p. 197 *Recent research in the neuroeconomics of trust*: Paul J. Zak, "The Neuroeconomics of Trust," in *Renaissance in Behavioral Economics: Essays in Honour of Harvey Leibenstein*, ed. Roger S. Frantz (Abingdon, UK: Routledge, 2007), 17–33.

p. 197 *The more powerful the emotional engagement*: Paul J. Zak, *The Moral Molecule: The Source of Love and Prosperity* (New York: Penguin, 2012).

p. 202 *"composing a life"*: Mary Catherine Bateson, *Composing a Life* (New York: Grove Atlantic, 2007).

p. 202 *"to look at problems"*: Bateson, *Composing a Life*, 16.

p. 202 *Deborah Price, founder of the Money Coaching Institute*: Deborah L. Price, *Money Magic: Unleashing Your True Potential for Prosperity and Fulfillment* (Novato, CA: New World Library, 2010).

Chapter 10: Unconditional Acceptance

p. 213 *we are literally the sum of our shared stories*: Jerome Bruner, *Acts of Meaning: Four Lectures on Mind and Culture* (Cambridge, MA: Harvard University Press, 1993).

p. 214 *offering unconditional acceptance has been useful*: I initially learned this practice while participating in a larger body of work focused on embodied spirituality that was facilitated by two Spanish teachers, Ramon Albareda and Marina Romero. In general, their work has provided an important inspiration for the embodied practices in this book.

p. 216 *the happiest person on the planet*: Matthieu Ricard, *Happiness: A Guide to Developing Life's Most Important Skill*, trans. Jesse Browner (New York: Little, Brown, 2006). Matthieu Ricard is a French-born Buddhist monk who has worked with neuroscientists to measure his brain waves. The results showed an uncharacteristically high capacity for happiness and reduced tendency toward negativity.

p. 217 *Your level of emotional intelligence*: Daniel Goleman, *Emotional Intelligence*, 25th anniv. ed. (London: Bloomsbury, 2020), ix.

p. 218 *"hijacked"*: John Mordechai Gottman and Julie Schwartz Gottman, *Fight Right: How Successful Couples Turn Conflict into Connection* (New York: Harmony, 2023), 27.

p. 222 *Mark Wolynn explores the science of epigenetics*: Mark Wolynn, *It Didn't Start with You: How Inherited Family Trauma Shapes Who We Are and How to End the Cycle* (New York: Penguin, 2017).

p. 223 *"offspring of severely stress-exposed parents"*: Mallory E. Bowers and Rachel Yehuda, "Intergenerational Transmission of Stress in Humans," *Neuropsychopharmacology* 41, no. 1 (2016): 232.

p. 223 *Healthy relationships can act as a buffer*: Bowers and Yehuda, "Intergenerational Transmission of Stress," 241.

Chapter 11: Entering the Money Lifeworld

p. 235 *"Being an ego through the living body"*: Edmund Husserl, *The Crisis of European Sciences and Transcendental Phenomenology: An Introduction to Phenomenological Philosophy*, trans. David Carr (Evanston, IL: Northwestern University Press, 1970), 108.

p. 237 *We matter because we are matter*: Maurice Merleau-Ponty, *The Visible and the Invisible*, trans. Alphonso Lingis (Evanston, IL: Northwestern University Press, 1968).

p. 237 *Our sensory experience of the environment*: David Abram, *The Spell of the Sensuous: Perception and Language in a More-Than-Human World* (New York: Pantheon Books, 1996).

p. 249 *the concept of somatic experiencing*: Peter A. Levine, *Waking the Tiger: Healing Trauma* (Berkeley, CA: North Atlantic Books, 1997).

Conclusion

p. 259 *"tiny mighty"*: Carolyn Buck Luce, *Epic! The Women's Power Play Book* (Austin: Lioncrest Publishing, 2022), 149–52.

ABOUT THE AUTHOR

Elizabeth Husserl is a speaker, registered investment advisor, and wealth planner who expertly guides people to a deeper understanding of their relationship to money and wealth. More than anything, she loves her life and fills her days with meaningful conversations, rituals, spreadsheets, and dancing.

Elizabeth is cofounder of Peak360 Wealth Management, a comprehensive boutique wealth planning firm in the San Francisco Bay Area. She leads her clients through a process that is equal parts financial planning, self-awareness, and practical implementation. Elizabeth champions her clients and empowers them to practice financial strategies that can generate greater wealth in the form of well-being.

Elizabeth holds Series 6, 63, and 65 licenses; a BS in economics from Tulane University; and an MA in East–West psychology from the California Institute of Integral Studies. She has been certified as a money coach by the Money Coach Institute. Elizabeth has presented at conferences and seminars including Wisdom 2.0 Los Angeles, Generational Group conferences in Colombia and Peru, and the Indaba Owners Conference, and she has led workshops at such leading tech companies as Airbnb, Unity, Google, and Amazon.

She lives with her husband, daughter, and two cats in the Bay Area, where she enjoys a vibrant and beloved community. She also calls New Orleans and Colombia home.